Alec McCowen writes as he acts, with compassion, precision and beauty. His memoir, **Young Gemini,** is funny, moving and full of discoveries and wonders. **Marian Seldes**

Young Gemini is a delightful memoir by the renowned British actor, Alec McCowen. Alec —his real name was Alexander, but his father said that it would be too expensive to put that up in lights—learned the art of acting at a very early age. The chief part, which he played with great success for many years, was that of the average schoolboy. But he also played— with, as he says, the utmost cynicism—the part of the traditional "little rascal." This role was received with acclaim, except by his father, who had an acute awareness of over-playing.

It was his father who dominated Alec's formative years, and whose death inspired this book. Deeply embedded in their relationship are the roots of Alec McCowen's acting career. His father was a richly eccentric man, given to outbursts of rage that passed like summer lightning. Mr. McCowen felt he had a private line to Jesus Christ, and was always expecting

Young Gemini

Alec McCowen

YOUNG
GEMINI

ATHENEUM
NEW YORK
1979

Library of Congress Cataloging in Publication Data

McCowen, Alec.
    Young Gemini.

    1. McCowen, Alec.   2. Actors—Great Britain—
Biography.   I. Title.
PN2598.M17A33   792'.028'0924 [B]   79-1991
ISBN 0-689-11004-9

For Mary

"Strange eclipse, when the hue of truth comes shadowing over our bright ideal planet."

GEORGE MEREDITH

". . . all that David Copperfield kind of crap."

J. D. SALINGER

Preface

I T seems as if American actors are the heroes of this story.

Or more specifically, that Marlon Brando, Jessica Tandy and the original cast of *A Streetcar Named Desire* are the heroes of this story.

For *Young Gemini* describes my acting journey from early childhood disguises, through adolescent exhibitionism, to that first encounter with actors who both challenged and inspired me.

It is over thirty years since *Streetcar*, but in the autumn of 1978, at a matinee in Boston, I saw Jessica Tandy playing with her husband, Hume Cronyn, in *The Gin Game*. Their performances moved me to tears. Once again I was a student actor—challenged and inspired.

Young Gemini was prompted by the death of my father. He died in August 1969, at the time

I was playing the title role in *Hadrian VII* in New York. The book was written a few months after that, when I was playing Hamlet in England with the Birmingham Rep.

When it was completed, I sent it to a couple of publishers. They both liked it, but said that it was too short, and suggested that I extend it into a full-length autobiography.

I didn't feel inclined to do this—chiefly because my writing output averages about a hundred pages every five years; but also it didn't seem to me to be right.

Everything in the book is related to my father, and his effect on me while I was growing up. Even such events as my early trips to India and New York came about partly because of my desire to please him. It wasn't until my mid-twenties, after my visit to *Streetcar*, that I really began to act independently.

But that's another story.

So I put this book away in a cupboard and almost forgot about it.

Then, in July 1978, I happened to read a very good review in *The Times* of a book called *Sorry, Dad* by Edward Blishen. It sounded as if it covered some of the same ground as my own story, and I bought a copy.

It is the most delightful book about growing up that I have ever read. In fact I was so touched and amused by Edward Blishen's writing that I wrote him a rare fan letter, mentioning that it was the sort of book I had once tried to write.

Mr. Blishen replied that he had admired my acting for many years, and sent me another of his books.

I wrote back and invited him and his wife to my solo performance of St Mark's Gospel, which was playing at the Comedy Theatre in London.

We met backstage for the first time.

In a couple of weeks Edward and Nancy invited me to their home for dinner. Nancy made a steak and kidney pie—and I nearly moved in.

Meanwhile Edward had mentioned my fan letter to his publisher, Christopher Sinclair-Stevenson. He—astonishingly—wrote to me, saying that if I had ever written anything he would like to see it. I pulled *Young Gemini* out of the cupboard, dusted it, re-read it, and sent it off with a covering note, admitting that it was far too short, but that I couldn't and wouldn't extend it.

Hamish Hamilton nonetheless accepted it. And now it is published in America by Atheneum.

———

In the ten years that have passed since my father's death, the family has continued to be influenced by him.

Within a couple of years, my sister decided that bringing up four children was not enough to satisfy her energy, and she took over the management of a huge Sue Ryder Home for the sick and disabled.

Last year, at the age of seventy, my mother announced that she was going to be confirmed.

And I find myself, taking time off from play acting, stomping around all over the place reciting St Mark's Gospel—and worrying if the audience doesn't laugh at the funny parts.

My father would have laughed at the funny parts . . .

He laughed a lot.

Young Gemini

S TANDING on a platform in the wings of the famous little theatre, waiting for my cue to come on stage and launch into "To be or not to be," I felt an unnatural fatigue and depression. I didn't care about Hamlet's problems. I didn't care about Hamlet's dead father. It was no concern of mine if his mother had married his uncle. Good luck to her!

These thoughts went through my mind at a moment that is supposed to be one of the summits of an actor's career. I had made a long journey to get on to that high platform. Twenty-five years ago I had played Francisco and Guildenstern in a repertory production and had hardly dared to dream that one day I might play the Prince of Denmark.

And now it didn't seem to matter.

I even seemed to resent it.

Why should I relinquish me and think and speak and feel for someone else?

To play a part successfully, half the work consists in understanding the character you're playing; to understand it in your own terms and relate it to your own experience. But nearly always the situations and the relationships actually belong to him and not to you. They belong to a puppet imagined by a playwright; and the actor is both pimp and prostitute.

Only occasionally the situation of the character collides with a similar situation in the actor's life. If this has been digested the parallel may be helpful. But sometimes the situations coincide and the result is confusion.

I felt a feeling of confusion as I stood on that high platform, waiting to "enter reading" and say the best-known line in dramatic literature as if it was new-minted. I had to stifle a desire to hurl the book at the coughing audience, tear off the dreary black clothes and piss on Elsinore.

I F I could choose, where would I wish to be? Childhood.

A summer afternoon on Bookham Common, lying deep in the bracken, gazing at the blue sky and dreaming of the future. Feeling relaxed and confident and aware of the enormous possibilities of life.

Bookham Common, and the family at Bookham, my mother's family, represented a world of freedom and imagination and individuality. It was here that I became aware that certain things were beautiful. It was here that I became aware that choices could be made. It was here that I became aware of colour and space and texture.

We drank China tea in pale blue cups; my cousin and I would climb an accommodating maple tree; at breakfast there was porridge that stood up in the plate covered with demerara sugar and cream; on the Common there was the little railway tunnel, and the exciting noise

5

of electric trains on their way to London. And in the garden there was the little wooden studio where my Auntie Dodi and Uncle Jim used to paint.

Coming from our ugly little semi-detached home, near Tunbridge Wells, where my father struggled hard to earn a living with a pram shop, the discovery that people could lead their lives, even if they didn't actually earn their livings, by painting pictures, by doing something so seemingly useless and at the same time so gorgeously fulfilling, was very exciting to me. And lying in the bracken, I celebrated a future that my mind couldn't formulate; like the happiness immediately after an enjoyable but forgotten dream. Except that this pleasure was before the dream, and long, long before the reality.

––––––––––

My father, Duncan McCowen, was a man of immense humour and imagination, but very little education.

He left school when he was fourteen and was sent to work as a draper's assistant. Then, after a spell in the army of occupation in Germany in 1918–19, he lugged furniture about in a shop in Tunbridge, and finally started his own business, calling it "Duncan's Pram Shop," so as not to be confused with his father who owned "McCowen's Music Centre" next-door-but-one in Monson Road, Tunbridge Wells. Later he opened two more shops—one in Hastings and one in East Grinstead. He called them "The Largest Pram Stores in the South of England," which impressed me mightily.

My mother trained in a ballet school at Palmers Green—Alicia Markova was one of her fellow pupils. When my father first saw her she was singing and dancing—the soubrette—in a concert party called "The Blue Birds" on the Palace Pier at Hastings. She was seventeen and he was twenty-four. I understand that my father would sit in the front row night after night to watch her—sending a red rose back-stage with an invitation to meet him afterwards. They fell madly in love, and despite opposition from his family, who regarded the theatre with horror, they married.

I was born in Tunbridge Wells nine months later, on May 26, 1925. My mother's family at Bookham and my father's family at Hastings were overjoyed by the arrival of the first grandchild. I was golden-haired and very spoilt.

My parents were a handsome couple and, despite the worry of earning a living in those early days, I think it must have been a very happy home.

Then, four years later, I was sent to the Bookham grandparents for a mysterious holiday, and
on my return discovered my mother in bed with
another child. My sister Jean had arrived. It
was then that I began to act.

I was told that I must be pleased. So I smiled.
I was told that I must love her. So I kissed her. I
was told that now I was a brother. So my golden
curls were all chopped off. I was told that now
I was a "little man" and must protect my sister,
and I was furious. I had been number one. I had
been the favourite. And now, suddenly, I was
expected to be a member of an Ensemble and
not a Star. It was like being with the Royal
Shakespeare Company.

(And indeed, over thirty years later, when I
played the Fool in the Brook-Scofield *King Lear*,
I recalled this feeling of displacement. When the
King meets Edgar, in his disguise as Poor Tom,
he begins to neglect the Fool and hardly ad-
dresses another word to him.)

Of course my mother and father did not in-
tend me to feel this discontent. They were as
aware as the majority of parents of the problem,
and I am sure they did all in their power to
bolster my threatened importance. It was more
likely the busy aunts and over-zealous friends
and neighbours who instilled the germs of re-
sentment in the mind of a vain little boy.

Nevertheless my very demonstrative father now had a little girl he could pet, without the restraint of turning his son into a milksop. And I became aware, more than anything else, of the difference in sex. I particularly remember fits of temper at being made to wear a prickly grey shirt that chafed my neck. When I protested, my father would tell me that "this is what boys wear"; and then began a series of instructions to guide me towards being a "real boy."

I think my father hoped that I would personify everything "boyish," and he had the strange habit of calling me "the boys"—"Hello, the boys," "Come on, the boys"—as if I was a football team. Even after I grew up my father persisted in attempts to mould me into his idea of masculinity. He loved to take me to village pubs for "half a pint" and didn't really like my preference for a gin and tonic. On one occasion he taught me to play "shove halfpenny." When I said it was a boring game, he was shocked and saddened and told me it was something "men liked doing."

Gradually, of course, he accepted these vagaries and even became proud that I was "a character."

Until I was ten we lived in one half of a semi-detached house in a quiet little road in Pembury, Kent. There was half an acre of garden at the back, a small part of which was cultivated with flower beds, a rockery, and crazy paving. My father had the names and dates of birth of my sister and myself written in the concrete on two of the paving stones. Beyond the rockery the grass grew wild, and at the end of this little wilderness was "Alec's garden": a tiny plot where I tried to grow flowers and vegetables. (This is powerfully recalled whenever I see vividly illustrated seed packets in a shop.) But mostly I used "my garden" as an escape from the family and to day-dream.

In the other half of our semi-detached lived my father's sister Maisie and her husband, Arthur Bush. They eventually had a daughter whom they called Heather Bush. (At Christmas, when singing "Good King Wenceslas," instead of "Hither page and stand by me" my sister would substitute the words "Heather Bush and stand by me.")

On the other side lived the Constables and their little daughter Anthea. Leslie Constable, who worked in a bank, was a superb pianist and, when I was eight, gave me my first piano lessons.

Beyond them, in a rather grander house, lived my friend Joycie Hayward. Her father owned the local bus company. They had peaches in their fruit bowl, and often had chicken for lunch. We only had chicken on very great occasions.

Chicken was a great luxury in the Thirties.

When I was five I went to the village school—about which I can remember very little except the lavatory at the bottom of the playground. This must have been a roofless affair as we boys used to try—and often succeeded—in peeing over our wall into the girls' side. I also remember the humiliation of lining up with the entire school to have my head inspected for lice.

On Sundays I went to the Free Church Sunday School, and learnt to palm the penny my parents had given me for the collection. We would parade past a black velvet bag, singing:

"Dropping, dropping, dropping, dropping,
Hear the pennies fall . . .
Every one for Jesus,
He shall have them all."

Except that he didn't have mine. I would dip my hand into the bag, hold on to my penny, and afterwards go to the village sweetshop and buy liquorice and sherbet. This shop was called "Lambert's," and my sister and I imagined the owners had a wonderful time eating all the sweets. (In fact, when singing the hymn "To be a Pilgrim," my sister would substitute the word "To be a Lambert.")

11

As a small boy I was somewhat tormented by
God and Jesus. We were taught at Sunday School
that "God is everywhere." I often woke up in the
night terrified that He was in the room. I would
force myself to look behind the dressing-table
mirror to see if He was there. We were told that,
if we were in any trouble, we had only to whisper
the name "Jesus" and the trouble would disap-
pear . . . it didn't. But especially I felt guilty
that the character of "Gentle Jesus, meek and
mild" seemed so unattractive to me. This image
was not helped by ghastly biblical pictures of a
pale little boy with a halo, a nightshirt, and a lot
of sheep. Luckily these fears and confusions were
soon dispelled by my father's superbly irreverent
attitude to formal Christianity. (And yet again
my sister. She had difficulty with the Holy
Trinity. "Father, Son and Holy Ghost" became
"Father, Son and . . . that other one.")

Despite the early jealousy, my sister and I
became good friends, and were able to amuse or
console each other with our cool clinical view
of the family scene. She was also my first audience.

When I was about seven, I ran into the road to
pick up a large shiny conker and was knocked
down by a car. I was carried home unconscious,
badly cut and bruised and with a minor head
injury. During convalescence, my mother's sis-

ter, Dodi, the artist, made me a model theatre. With this, and with the aid of evil-smelling coloured light bulbs, I devised a strange entertainment. The climax of the entertainment was a scene in which a naked headless doll was covered in a shower of Robertson's Marmalade paper golliwogs. On wet afternoons my sister was forced to watch this—but on one occasion during a rather lethargic performance, I looked to see her reaction, and discovered her reading a book. I had a fit of temperament and the performance ended in tears.

I think in later years the memory of this disaster led me towards a tendency to over-act— especially at matinees.

I think we must have known someone who worked for Robertson's Marmalade. As well as my huge store of paper golliwogs—there were thousands of them—I started a "Golliwog Club."

This was held on one evening a week during the summer. There were about twenty members drawn from the neighbouring village children. I had a roll call, and a large book where I marked attendance and absence. My mother made golliwog badges and provided snacks. If it was fine, we played in the garden, otherwise the club was trapped in our little dining room and I read to them. I preferred this. But after a series of wet evenings, attendance dwindled, and the run was terminated. I must have been a tyrant because, if golliwogs misbehaved, they were punished. One evening, long after the members had gone home and I had gone to bed, my mother heard distant crying coming from outside. She went to investigate and found a shivering little girl standing in the corner at the far end of the garden. I had banished her during the evening, and then forgotten her.

Both my parents were exuberant performers. Although my mother never returned to the stage, she would often sing as she dressed or did the housework. And, before leaving for the pram shop, my father loved to conduct the "Hallelujah Chorus." He played a record of this on the Gramophone and stood facing the mirror, waving his arms and shouting at the choir to "Sing up you buggers!"

My first attempt at a public performance was ignominious. I was often taken to a Concert Party in the park. One week there was a talent competition held for the children. We were to learn a song or poem and to be judged by the amount of applause we received. I worked hard at my number—I think it was a rendition of "Tiptoe Through the Tulips." But, when the time came for me to mount the stage, I refused and wouldn't budge from my seat. It wasn't stage fright. I couldn't bear *not* to win, and wouldn't risk defeat.

(As a young actor I never minded auditions —except when there were other actors waiting in the wings. All I could think of was the opinion of my colleagues, and so I courted defeat.)

My earliest visit to a proper theatre was to a matinee of the local amateur Operatic Society in *Rose Marie*. For some forgotten reason, at the last moment my parents were unable to accompany me, so I was parked in my seat in the gallery and given my bus fare home. It was glorious. I was rapt in the wonder of it and, when the curtain came down and the lights came up, I fled from the theatre to hide my tears. My mother seemed surprised to see me home so soon —and then it transpired that in my innocence I had left at the intermission—amazed that the theatre should be such a tragic place. I have never seen the second half of *Rose Marie* but whenever I hear the "Indian Love Call," I recall stumbling down the gallery stairs of the Opera House, Tunbridge Wells, weeping at my first encounter with unfulfilled love.

Later I saw productions by the amateurs of *Rio Rita*, *The Desert Song*, and *Chu Chin Chow* —all of them glorious—but I cannot remember

15

when I saw my first straight play. It must have seemed rather tame.

The Opera House was only used as a theatre by the Operatic Society, the Christmas Pantomime, and rare visits of those beloved concert parties the "Fol de Rols" and "Twinkle." Otherwise it was a cinema.

I loved "the pictures" and would beg my parents to take me every week. There was the Opera House, the Great Hall and the Kosmos; and later the sumptuous Ritz Cinema opened, complete with an illuminated glass organ which rose up and down on a lift and changed colours according to the moods of the music. A visit to the Ritz was enhanced by having tea in the Florida Café upstairs. There was also the thrill of seeing the local advertisements. After a plug for Gladys Wells, who sold corsets on The Pantiles, the commentator would say, "Up and down the hills of Tunbridge Wells go Duncan's Prams . . . Showrooms at 14, Monson Road."

My early idols were Jack Hulbert and Cicely Courtneidge, the North Country comedian Sydney Howard, and the pop-eyed American entertainer Eddie Cantor. I went into raptures over Cantor's musical films *Roman Scandals*, *The Kid from Spain* and *Kid Millions*, and gasped at the beauty of the Goldwyn Girls. I also adored Jack

Buchanan, and wept whenever I heard him sing "Goodnight Vienna." I would do anything to be taken to the pictures, and one summer helped a family at hop-picking, on the firm understanding that a certain number of bushels picked would mean a free trip to see Elisabeth Bergner in *Catherine the Great*. My bedroom was decorated with glossy photographs of Janet Gaynor, Fredric March, Joan Crawford and William Powell, and my pocket money was spent on buying *The Picturegoer* and *Film Show* magazines. But I think my greatest pleasure was derived from a collection of Gramophone records made by the Cinematograph Trade Benevolent Fund called "The Voice of the Stars." These were recorded excerpts from the sound tracks of current films. There were about half a dozen of these records and I knew them all by heart. I can still recite many of the scenes and frequently burst into terrible impersonations of Charles Laughton in *The Barretts of Wimpole Street* and *Mutiny on the Bounty*; George Arliss in *Voltaire*; Norma Shearer and Fredric March in *Smilin' Thru*; and especially Ronald Colman and Loretta Young . . . "I've given my life for India. It's taken one of my children. He's dead! Dead, and for what? . . ." from *Clive of India*.

I don't know when I first decided that I wanted

to be an actor, but I cannot remember ever wanting to be anything else. However, it was not for
many years that I admitted this to my father.

———————

When I was eight, I was sent to The Skinner's
School in Tunbridge Wells—and became, according to the local joke, a "Skinner Rabbit."
This was a big Grammar School with about four
hundred pupils. It was built in red brick, and
had a large Hall with Gothic windows.

The week before term started, my father took
me for a drive and gave me a very feeble "sex
talk"—not wanting me to be at a disadvantage
with my more sophisticated classmates. The talk
only covered the fact of babies growing inside
mothers—and I felt sure that he had left out a
great deal. But, being a very sensitive boy, I was
aware of his embarrassment at discussing the
matter at all, so I didn't press him further. In
any case his embarrassment transferred itself
to me, and I felt sure it must be a dirty and
delightful subject.

It was not long before a boy at the new school
told me what men and women actually did together. This was traditionally told in a dark
corner behind "the bogs." My reaction was to

consider it extremely childish and undignified. It did not occur to me to associate my own secret masturbation with these strange contortions. And anyway I couldn't see how my father's limp old dangler would *go* into *anything*.

My first day at school was very uncomfortable as I was too nervous to ask where the lavatories were situated. I heard mention of "the bogs" but this meant nothing to me. As the day wore on, I thought my bladder would burst—and this was not helped by a Gym Class in the late afternoon. Finally we were dismissed; and then my father didn't turn up to take me home. I can still remember standing miserably by the school gates, my satchel laden with strange books—we had been told to read the first chapter of our literature book for home-work and, as I didn't know what the word literature meant, I took home everything—and piddling discreetly through my short trousers, trying to miss my brand-new shoes and socks.

After the first day things got better, and I was delighted to make a great new friend, called Dicky Miles who also lived in Pembury—especially as he was always bottom of the class, saving me from this position. I was next to bottom. He was a very cheerful, pugnacious boy and soon became popular with the entire school —who nicknamed him "Carnera," after the huge

Italian boxer. I was also quite aggressive, and one day, after I accidentally hit him in the eye with my gym vest while changing, we had a violent fight. To my great astonishment, I won. Everyone in the class, including myself, was extremely embarrassed by this victory, as it was unthinkable that "Carnera" could be beaten. I was appalled at the prospect of losing his friendship but, when the time came to go home, he calmly put his arm through mine as if nothing had happened. I was amazed and deeply moved by this, and had my first intimations that the race is not necessarily to the swift, nor the battle to the strong; and I loved Dicky Miles.

At this distance in time it is difficult to reconcile and understand the aggressive and passive phases of my boyhood. Sometimes at school I was known as a terror and went looking for fights. But there were times when I would run away and avoid conflict, and my father feared I was a coward and not "a real boy." The truth seems to lie in a strange assumption that boys who came from working-class backgrounds—and there were many of them at the school—were bound to be tougher than me, and I was physically afraid of them. In any case it didn't seem right to add to their hardships by beating them, and in my guilt I carefully avoided conflict—

while exaggerating their stamina. There was obviously an association with my father, whom I
often saw when he got home from work, tired
and dirty from lifting, repairing and delivering
prams. He appeared to me a colossus of strength.
How could *I* hit *him?* Like most sons I was in
awe of my father's strength; but, unlike most
sons, it seemed unthinkable ever to compete
with it. And anything he could do, I assumed
I could *not* do better.

My most vivid early memory is standing on
my grandparents' lawn at Hastings watching
my father throw a ball so high in the sky that
it vanished from sight . . . Not once, but again
and again . . . I have never been able to throw
a ball with any strength. I have always assumed
it to be impossible. It was the same with football. My father had been an avid player and
often talked lovingly about it. I was a hopeless
player. On the other hand, I was a star at gym-
nastics, and a very carefree cricketer—in neither
of which my father had much experience.

The only time we played happily together was
a game of our own devising called "The King's
Game"—in which we were equally matched.
This was played by hitting a tennis ball against
the side of the house for the largest number
of hits. Since the ball would bounce off window-

sills and drainpipes, and often land in the middle of the rose-bed, it was quite difficult. My father would say "The King says we must do it twenty times in succession or else—" and then he would devise some terrible imaginary punishment . . . it would rain on our summer holidays, or my sister's guinea-pig would die, or my mother would go bald . . . This lent immense savour to the game. I can't remember that the King ever rewarded us for winning.

I was a happy enough schoolboy, although quite early I realised that it was a waste of time and something that had to be done for convention's sake. The majority of subjects were not remotely interesting to me and most of the others I could have taught myself at home. It seemed mad to spend so much time on Latin, or Algebra, or Physics, if you were not going to concentrate your life on these subjects. Nothing was taught about health; nothing was taught about the law; nothing was taught about money. And, like many people, I am constantly regretting my ignorance about these things.

However, we had quite good English masters and I got a fair introduction to Shakespeare— indeed Mr Smith, who loved to read aloud, was one of the best Rosalinds I have ever heard.

And I adored Geography.

My first actual experience of the difference between places and people sprang from journeys
with my parents to the scrubby chalk countryside of Surrey and the pebbly-beached seaside
of Sussex: to my mother's questioning, political
and artistic family at Bookham, and my father's
emotional, religious and philistine family at
Hastings. A great deal of my childhood was spent
in holidays with my maternal and paternal
grandparents. They were vastly different house-
holds—and extremely colourful.

It is very hard for me to believe my memories
of the family at Hastings. They belong to another century.

The house was thickly curtained. There was
stained glass in the hall and in the lavatory;
there was a harmonium; huge glass cabinets
packed with ornaments; watery pictures of High-
land cattle; a hot and damp conservatory which
seemed to be part of the sitting-room; and a
dining-room table covered with a baize cloth, a
heavy tablecloth with tassels, and on top of these
a linen cloth for meal times. I can still remember
secretly plaiting the tassels while waiting for my
food.

There was a faithful old maid-servant called

Benson—who could cut slices of bread and butter
so thin that there seemed to be more butter than
bread. Benson "lived in," and had a private back
staircase to her bedroom.

My father's family had ostracised my parents
until I was born. Then pride in the first grandchild overcame their terror of my mother's past
connection with the stage, and she was allowed
into their home.

Grandpa McCowen was described in his obit-
uary in the *Hastings and St. Leonard's Observer*
as "one of the leading evangelists in the South of
England . . . He began his work of evangelism
at 18 and had spoken from more than 300 pulpits.
In all his work for 50 years he had the support
of his wife, particularly on the musical side. A
man of vital personality and lovable character,
he linked up with all Christian effort and took
services in any church irrespective of denomina-
tion." As a red-haired young man he had been a
commercial traveller, and then a highly successful shopkeeper. He loved to preach and he loved
to eat. When I knew him he weighed about 250
pounds.

A traditional part of a holiday in Hastings was
a visit with my grandpa to Cave's Café for morning coffee. Here we met an old friend of his,
Mr Plumbridge, who was a good listener. On
one occasion my grandpa told his friend of a

visitation during the previous night from God
Himself. I listened spellbound to this informa-
tion, but Mr Plumbridge did not seem greatly
surprised. Then there followed the usual joke
with the waitress of my being given the bill, a
slow walk along the front, and the journey home
crushed against my grandpa in the trolley bus
and another joke with the conductor about my
paying the fare.

Grandma McCowen was a tiny woman who
"particularly supported him on the musical side"
by her talents at the piano, harmonium and
organ. Although her hands shook alarmingly, she
played hymns with a passion and strength which
thrilled me to the marrow. She was a great performer, and a Christmas visit to "Glenthorne"
was not complete without a gathering round the
piano of my father's three sisters; their husbands;
my great aunt Madge; my father's younger
brother; my grandfather, my parents and myself. Later we were joined by my sister, and
cousins Heather, Dan and "Little O." We would
belt out "Guide me O Thou Great Jehovah,"
"There Is a Green Hill Far Away," "Christian!
seek not yet repose," and other favourites. (Before a trip to Hastings my poor stage-soiled
mother, who dreaded these occasions, would
learn the words of several hymns so that she
could join in with the others during Grandma's

"request time.") I enjoyed it enormously.

I also enjoyed a grace which we sang before special meals:

"Be present at our table Lord!
Be here and everywhere adored!
These mercies bless and grant that we
May feast in Paradise with thee."

—although it struck me as a rather gluttonous idea.

One Christmas, of blessed memory, my father's sister Gladys—or "Glad-eyes" as she was affectionately called—told us a story with lantern slides, called "How the Littlest Camel came to see the Infant Jesus." The reverential atmosphere was too much for me. I disgraced myself by laughing and had to leave the room.

On another occasion, aged about seven, I personally gave a cabaret consisting of impersonations of the band conductor Henry Hall, the film star George Arliss, and the variety team called the Western Brothers. One of my stories concerned a parrot and a canary who were kept, for some obscure reason, in a bathroom. A beautiful lady arrived to take a bath. The canary said, "Peep peep. Peep peep." To which the parrot replied: "You can peep if you want to; I'm going to have a damn good look." There was a startled

silence from my audience, and on this occasion
I think my mother had to leave the room.

In addition to the hymn singing and the family
prayers, I associate a great deal of actual physical
contact with the family at Hastings. There was
always a lot of hugging and kissing and sitting
on laps. The girls—as my large aunts were called
—would walk around with arms entwined. My
little grandmother had a hypnotic trick of sitting
very close; slowly raising and lowering a deli-
cately chained pendant in front of one's eyes;
making a strange soft clicking noise with her
tongue; and then suddenly and violently tickling
one's ribs with the shaky but steely fingers of
her free hand. My sister and I were both fascinated and repelled by this game, and would
sometimes play it with each other.

My big grandfather loved to get me on his
knee—or in his bed—and recite:

> *"Mary had a little lamb*
> *Its fleece was black as soot*
> *And everywhere that Mary went*
> *His sooty foot he put."*

This always culminated in a splutter and
squeal of giggles, and an attack of tickles much
heavier than my grandmother's. Sometimes the
tickles even hurt.

Finally there was my father's teenage brother, whose assaults on me were of a far more sadistic nature.

The combined impression of these extraordinary people—the hypnotic smiles, the hymn singing, the gluttony, and the heavy sexual undertones, made a heady mixture for a little boy. I found it both funny and frightening. The thing that puzzled me most was their complacency, and their blithe intolerance of most of the outside world. George Eliot's marvellous description of professional Christians would have fitted them completely: "They really look on the rest of mankind as a doomed carcase which is to nourish them for heaven."

A holiday at Bookham opened up very different areas for my young imagination.

Here I could listen to Gramophone records of Schnabel playing Beethoven Sonatas; hilarious stories of some funny men called the Marx Brothers; and my grandfather talking endlessly about the French Revolution. Here the family often quarrelled, meals were late, and, unlike the Hastings household, it was very difficult to get into the bathroom as they seemed to take baths at all times of the day.

When we arrived, my grandfather might be at the top of the garden with his game-cocks and chickens, Uncle Jim would be painting in the studio, Auntie Dodi would be in the bath, cousin John up a tree, and my little auntie Peggy battling with a complicated menu in the kitchen. Eventually, after much shouting and laughter, we would all assemble round the dining-room table. There would be cider and beer, and cousin John would be told to go and wash his hands, and my mother and Dodi would implore Peggy to sit down and stop fussing, and my grandfather and uncle Jim would embark on a political argument, and I would watch my father—who felt as ill at ease in this household as my mother did at Hastings.

My father had as much intelligence and humour as any of them—and much more sense—but he lacked education and could easily be annihilated by my grandfather quoting Carlyle or my uncle extolling Cézanne. But at least they did not talk down to him, and over the years they were often in his debt for help in practical matters—about which they were frequently inept.

My maternal grandfather was called Alex-

ander George Walkden and I was named after
him. He told me that he had been named after
the actor George Alexander—but I worked out
the dates of birth and discovered he must have
been romancing. A pity! He was a beautiful,
small, bearded man, and he has an important
place in the history of the Trade Union Move-
ment. He was a founder of the Railway Clerks
Association, and was their General Secretary for
thirty years. He became Labour MP for South
Bristol and was a member of the Long Parliament of 1935–45. Then, in order to strengthen
the Labour majority in the House of Lords, he
became a peer, Lord Walkden, Baron of Great
Bookham. To help supplement his income—
which was not enough to support the Bookham
household—the Prime Minister Clement Attlee
also made him the second Government Whip,
and the Captain of the King's Bodyguard of the
Yeomen of the Guard. He served successfully in
the Lords for a few years and then, suddenly,
his brain collapsed and he finished his days in a
home at Virginia Water. When I visited him
there he said his devotion to Socialism had been
a mistake and his life a failure . . . Also, after
a lifetime of serving the railways, he was afraid
to go on a train lest he should lose his luggage.

My Grandma Walkden died when I was too
young really to remember her, and my grand-

father was very lonely. He confided in me about this one evening when we were out walking, and I felt very flattered and grown-up. But I also felt the ghastly panic of being unable to comfort him. Dodi and Jim did not help matters with their absorption in painting and total indifference to financial matters. Both they and my grandfather had quick tempers and it was not a restful household.

But it was here that I first became aware of myself, and it was here that I developed a critical faculty and built up a protective wall to safeguard the alarming love and anger growing inside me.

There was a most extraordinary game, played by my sister, my cousin John and myself, which I could not have devised anywhere but at Bookham. It was called "Angels"—and it quietly mocked birth, religion, life, death and resurrection. It was a potted version of the human cycle, and gave great opportunities for dramatic death falls, followed by a slow motion heavenly life (wrapped up in old sheets) and then, when heaven became boring, a flower-like rebirth. We played it for hours on the lawn. I think it was an expression of my young impatience with the mumbo-jumbo of adults, and with their lack of simple direct enjoyment in the obvious miracles of life.

31

The strong personalities at Bookham didn't smother me with love, but regarded me as an interesting growing person. When I think of childhood my first thoughts are always of those days —doubtless romanticised—when I felt a sense of freedom untroubled by the nagging necessities of being "a real boy" or a good boy, or a scholar or a son and heir. Here I was able to look and listen and absorb. The gnarled trunk of the oak tree in the garden; the bounce of the turf on the common; clouds rushing across a huge sky; and the distant noise of the trains on their way to London. Perhaps more than anything else I loved the little station, with its kiosk selling chocolate cream bars. It was an escape route. The shining metal rails disappearing into the promise of a world of adventure. I looked and planned and dreamed.

Reality has been better than the dream—and this book is in part a love-letter.

———

This book is also a search for an explanation; an explanation of the need I felt to disguise myself. This habit started, as I have already written, at the birth of my sister. Then it was necessary, since a child of four years is trapped by size and

age and is not fully articulate. He must comply—
or rage in absolute frustration. But when I grew
older I could possibly have talked about my
mystification with my father or my mother or
with the family at Bookham. Instead, the disguise grew greater.

The disguise was a smile; a readiness to agree;
a false good nature, a compliance with what I
thought was expected.

The mystification which I hid was the mystery
of my own personality, with my steadily forming
sense of taste and values. Should I reveal my dis-
gust at people and things that seemed to be accepted? Should I reveal a growing awareness
of beauty? Should I reveal that my nature seemed
to be part masculine, part feminine? Should I
reveal my cowardice? Should I reveal a desire to
blow up the house, the school, the shop, the
street, the garden, the neighbours, the family?
Should I reveal the love of my father which was
stifled by his impatience for me to become a
"real boy"? Should I—*could* I—criticise God?

What was a miracle?

What was a prayer?

And what the hell was horse-power? My father
often mentioned it.

I was too afraid to talk about these things.

Why was I afraid?

There was guilt of course.

33

A large element of this came from masturbation. The family, especially my father, made endless references to the bladder and the bowels. There was a plethora of lavatory-jokes, and jokes about urinating, wind and defecation. But there was never a reference to sex. This was astonishing and impossible to understand. For years I thought my powers of erection were unique. For years I thought that I had stumbled on a gorgeous secret known only to me—and perhaps the angels. Since I had this pleasure, how could I criticise the poor deprived common herd of humanity? I had better keep quiet or someone might take it away.

But perhaps more deeply I was afraid of my own personality; afraid of my critical faculty; my impatience; and afraid of my vain belief in my intelligence and genius. This was a hangover from being the number one golden-haired child who astonished everyone—simply by being alive and well and living in Tunbridge Wells. He had only to lie in his pram and the world came to praise him and love him and pay their respects. It had been so easy. A gurgle would delight them and a tiny clenched fist amaze them. Then, suddenly, the golden-haired days were over, and I had to struggle to become the "real boy," the schoolboy, the conforming boy. And I did not believe in that struggle. I didn't think it necessary.

Basically I knew that the golden-haired genius was still underneath the close-cut brown-haired, average-looking, dreary schoolboy. But nobody was interested. They wanted something else. So I started the disguise. And this led to acting.

The chief part I played for many years was the part of an average schoolboy. I managed—after the early days of being bottom of the class with Dicky Miles—to be somewhere in the middle of the class. To be average height, average weight and of average personality (except to a few select friends). My ambition was to leave school without anybody noticing that I had been there—and to my delight I nearly achieved this. When I said good-bye to one of the masters who had taught me for nearly eight years, he had great difficulty in remembering my name. I nearly congratulated him.

I also played—with the utmost cynicism—the part of the traditional "little rascal." Charming and potentially "naughty." I played this part to perfection at Hastings where I knew my grandparents liked me to eat lots of cakes and have pockets bursting with string and conkers and boyish paraphernalia. Sometimes I even specially dirtied my hands and knees. It was an artful performance, but after one very successful visit to tea with my grandmother, when I had overplayed the role and eaten far too many cakes and grinned far too expertly—making full use of a new gap in my teeth—my father commented on my performance and mimicked me. I was amazed at his perception. It was the first time anyone had found me out. I blushed to the roots of my carefully tousled hair.

But mostly I succeeded in my performances, and this led to an enjoyment of them. I decided to bide my time. Let the schooldays pass. Soon there would be more enjoyable parts to play. And there would be lights and make-up and applause. I started to draw theatre scenes in my school books—mostly of audiences waiting for the curtain to rise. Rows and rows of people. There was never an empty seat . . .

Meanwhile, the secretive, bloody-minded, phoney youngster carried on with everyday scenes of family and school life.

———————

In 1935, when I was ten, my father's finances must have improved because we moved to a bigger house, in Langton Green, on the other side of Tunbridge Wells.

There was an acre of garden and we had a young gardener called William. He must have been very patient for I was fond of telling him the plots of all the films I had seen. *Wuthering Heights* went on for hours. We also had a glamorous maid called Joan, who slept above me in the top room.

It was the sort of house that children draw, set in the middle of the garden, square and red-tiled—called, in fact, "Red Tiles." There was a lawn with a border of rose trees. There were two larch trees, a beautiful beech tree, an oak tree that I used to climb, and an old medlar tree. There was a vegetable garden, and there were two sheds—one for my bicycle and the garden tools, and one for my sister's rabbits and guinea pig. We were screened from the road by a high hedge of rhododendrons, and there was a drive.

For the first time I had my own bedroom and my father bought a piano. Also, to fill a new bookcase, I asked him for a second-hand edition of the works of Dickens. He bought forty-eight volumes of the Waverley Novels instead—I suppose because there were more of them. I tried to hide my disappointment but, apart from *Ivanhoe*, they gathered dust.

To encourage my piano playing, my mother bought me some cheap busts of Beethoven, Schubert and Chopin, and these gazed down at me from the top of a cupboard—competing with the latest glossy photographs of Garbo, Spencer Tracy and Fred Astaire, who gazed at me from the mantelpiece.

We were all delighted by the change of scene —though it meant leaving good friends at Pembury: Dicky Miles with the house he had built in a tree, Joycie Hayward with her peaches on the sideboard, and Peter Curd with his farm where one could eat unlimited strawberries. But I had a stimulating new school-friend, John Gower, who loved to argue, who shared my humour, and whom I strongly suspected of being more intelligent. Unlike me—now playing the average schoolboy—he was a very good scholar and was not afraid to shine. He was also radiantly honest, and when an entire class lied to the master about some unaccomplished scripture homework—"I had toothache"—"My mother was ill"—"I left it on the bus"—etc.—John Gower just said, "I didn't do it." We were awed by his bravery although it enraged us. I think he reminded me of my father.

The days became a pattern. My sister and I would get up at 7:30, quarrel over the use of the wash-basin, and have breakfast with my mother and Joan in the kitchen. My father invariably stayed in bed and usually remained there till I bicycled to school at 8:30—even though his shop opened at 9 o'clock. Sometimes, if it was raining hard, he would get up and drive me into Tunbridge Wells—but even this did not always happen. One day, when he would not get up, I remember standing in a downpour shouting up at his bedroom window, "You lazy sod!"—trembling at my effrontery. He couldn't bear for *me* to lie in bed. And if I did so—on Sundays or holidays—he would shout from his room, "Get up my son! Get out of bed! You're rotting! You'll lie there and rot!" Sometimes he would even come and tear the covers off me, and then return to bed himself.

School began at 9 o'clock with a fifteen-minute service in the Hall. This was theatrical and I enjoyed it. Mr Mabbat played the organ with dramatic effect and John Gower and I looked for double meanings in the hymns and psalms. As there were not enough chairs to go round, some of us sat on the pipes—which in the winter got very hot—and there was a good deal of wriggling during the lesson. At the end of term we sang "Now thank we all our God" and "Jerusalem," which I found deeply moving.

Then classes began and monotony followed. I think more than anything else I learnt a sense of time. Of course there were diversions. The desks were in pairs and it helped to have an amusing partner. These varied from classroom to classroom. John Gower refused to sit with me because I made him inattentive. But occasionally I found a kindred spirit to help while away the time with grimaces behind the master's back, defacing pictures in books, and—when I was older—sex.

During the break there was either a rush to the bogs or a rush to the milk and bun queue. Then John Gower and I would play some bizarre game—like "The Kangaroo." One of us was a kangaroo and the other its owner. The owner had to get the kangaroo into the cricket nets or some enclosure. The kangaroo was allowed to kick. Once a fossil of a master caught us at the game and said, "Put up your hands and fight like men." It was useless to explain, so John Gower and I obliged—and quietly marvelled at the unimaginative world of old men.

Sometimes I had a "school dinner," but usually I bicycled home to Langton—two and a half miles away—for lunch with the family. Family meals—and especially lunch—were often dramatic occasions. My father was the star of these dramas.

He was frequently late—having stopped off at the pub for a drink—and my mother would be nervous about a spoilt meal. Then, when he arrived, everything had to be exactly right. I think memories of his own strict upbringing were stirred at meals-times. If a fork was missing there was trouble. If the vegetables were cold or the meat was tough or if something was dropped, there was more trouble. Discipline—not always evident—was suddenly enforced, and my father became a Victorian tyrant. We were told to sit up straight and put our shoulders back. I had round shoulders and it was hard for me. My father would call me "the cripple"—"Pass the gravy to the cripple"—"Give the hunchback some salt!—and don't answer back!" And then he demanded elegant conversation. My mother would nervously ask my sister or me some fatuous question about what we had learnt at school that morning, or where we would like to go on our holidays. And we would mutter or giggle and blush, and wish we were anywhere else. And then, suddenly, my father's mood would change and he would turn to the window and shout "get off the grass!" to some imaginary figure on the empty lawn, and the tension would ease. Then the meal would change from drama to comedy. My father would break wind, my sister and I would laugh, and my mother would start protesting ineffectually. My father once farted "God Save The King"—up to "Send him victorious." On another occasion, after a particularly pungent explosion, and my sister and I made for the door, my father stopped us. "Nobody is to leave the room," he shouted. "Give it a chance! You'll grow used to it!" It never ceased to amuse us. True to form, I had only an average talent, and, after a tentative effort, my father would ask, "Can't you do better than that?"— then there would be a desperate silence while Joan came in to clear the dishes and my father would resume his Victorian aspect. These changes of mood were bewildering and it is not surprising that we all suffered from indigestion.

There was a dreadful day when my sister dropped an entire apple pie on the floor. My father shouted at my sister. I shouted in protest at my father. My father shouted at me. My mother shouted at all of us. Several minutes of nervous silence followed until we all started to laugh uncontrollably and my father congratulated me. I had defended my sister. It was the act of a "real boy."

Then it was back to school for more lessons. Sport on Wednesday or Saturday, and Scouts on Monday. On my free afternoon I usually went to the pictures. I had a piano lesson once a week and for a little while I played the organ—practising in the village church. Sometimes I would play a selection from *Snow White and the Seven Dwarfs* and then, terrified lest someone was lurking in the dark shadows, would quickly revert to Sacred Music. At weekends we would often go to the Congregational Church. My other hobbies were bicycling, the model theatre, and climbing trees. In the evening there was homework and the radio.

———————

When I was eleven, twelve and thirteen—before the self-conscious years—I was a diligent diarist. I liked a particular type of scribbling diary because it had a blotter between each page where I could write general comments on myself, the family, and world news. Although, even at that age, I had an eye to posterity, and was also aware that the family might read it, there are some unguarded moments and small explosions of frustration which are both funny and revealing. Here is a selection from 1937, starting when I was eleven.

2 *May* (Sunday)
Climb oak tree in garden and couldent get down. Father got me in end.

3 *May*
Hottest day yet. Scouts in afternoon, go on common and do tracking which was awful and Hot. Get home. Mother in temper. In evening Father in temper. me fed up.

Alec McCowen

5 May

Cricket Hurray. Score "Duc" lovely day. (Spanish War still on since 1936 October)

12 May

Coronation Day. Get up 3 o clock all dark. Have a quike breakfast, my egg is bad. Get on train easily Father gets 1st class emty carriage. I saw most of Duchess of Glocester, bit of Duchess of Kent, Hon. Gerald Lascelles, Queen Mary, Princess Margaret Rose, bit of Princess Elizabeth, Then HURRAY THE KING AND QUEEN I saw them very well, the crowns as well. Finally go home, tell mum all about it. Later on we hear the king broadcast very s s s s stuteringly but he did it with grit. Then jolly good Variety. So endeth a day of days Amen.

6 June

Happy and unhappy day. In garden most of time, fall over and hurt myself. Ma and Pa in fairly good moods.

7 June

Scouts quite good but hot. Get Damn Sick and Fed up with Blasted Prep.

8 June

bit of rain. Music Lesson. Jean Harlow dies at 26. (Down with filthy Latin)

44

12 June
Pa in rotten mood. Go to T.W. in afternoon and try to get in to "Rembrant" (Opera House) but its an "A." BLAST IT.

4 July
In afternoon June and Jill Creamer come. Give concert with theatre, but as girls would they soon got tired of me.

24 July
School in morn fair. Dinner Ma and Pa in sarcastic tempers about me (blast 'em) DOWN WITH REARMAMENT

9 Aug.
In morn Gower comes. Muck about. In aft go to T.W. Open air Baths. Jolly good shute. Aunty Madge dies. New Pram Shop opens in T.W. DAMN called Pramcots.

13 Aug.
Mooch around stand outside Pramcots for 20 mins. No-one goes in. Ha Ha Ha. In eve posh game of Table Tennis with Joan. (DOWN WITH PRAMCOTS)

21 Aug.
(At Scout Camp) In eve a double damn good camp fire. Our patrol do stunt. me in sextet of

45

jazz songs and I by myself sing (or bawl) the "Cock Robin Opera," best applause. HAPPY.

27 Aug.
Robert Taylor film star comes to England. 2000 girls meet him. beaucoup de swoons.

6 Oct.
In aft go (with Ma and Pa) a la fleeks to see "LOST HORIZON" DM. good. 24 weeks run in London. Darn good scenery among Hymaleyas. (1008 miles on bike.)

14 Oct.
SKINNERS (B) DAY BLA BLA. 3.20 parade for Scouts wait ½ hour in B cold for D Governors. Then me in choir. Then P.T. display and Then Scouts display. And then home to finish off tea of Jeans Party after a Damn Day. (Feel Fed up with everything. Feel RESTLESS. WISH I was DOING something)

27 Oct.
Afternoon off. Wet out so have Theatre out. DAMN GOOD.

6 Dec.
(General News) King Leopold in England. Death of Ramsay MacDonald. The King goes

grouse shooting. Alec McCowen Future Great
Actor wants term to end.

———————

My 1938 diary started off with a warning in
huge letters underlined in red crayon.

To ALL readers THIS DIARY IS STRICTLY
PRIVATE. Any person looking at it does so at
his OWN RISK.

9 Jan 1938
Go to Bookham. HURRAY. Mess around common. Watch trains.

15 Jan
go to "Captains Courageous" Ritz. DARN GOOD
ENTERTAINMENT. Stay round and see some
again. Spencer Tracy Marvellous.

2 Feb.
In aft go with Pop to see "Good Earth." DARN
GOOD but not quite as good as expected.

19 Feb.
HAPPY. Half Hol. in aft Rest??!! THEN Skin-
ners School Scout Concert. Me in "Decoy"
Blinkin Girl part but everything goes tres damn

well. Place packed. Very happy. Parents Pleased. (Dad said I acted well HURRAY and could not get more out of the (blinkin) part. LOVE acting. Want to, and WILL)

5 *March*
Go and see "A STAR IS BORN" Best seen this year. Fredric March my favourite actor. Janet Gaynor very pretty. IN COLOUR. Story of Hollywood. (Place of my Dreams) Shall remember it for ever. DAMN GOOD. Scouts not much in eve.

10 *March*
Exams. French, Chem, Alg, and Geom. $4\frac{1}{2}$ hours of maddening torture. SCREAM!!!
Joan with measles. Father with temper. Jean with chill. Mother with the lot to look after. 158 miles on bike.
(Austria invaded by Germans. As good as won now Hitler, Goebbles there. Will it begin the World War that will HAVE to come?)

27 *March*
Sunday. Church in morn Boring. Ludo, Sweets, Piano etc. Stage Fever. Want to grow up.

30 *April*
The afternoon was occupied by listening to cup final won dramatically in the last $50\frac{3}{4}$ sec. and

lost lamentably by Huddersfield. Not that I'm interested in footer (I KNOW Mum and Dad do not want me to act on films or stage and think that I won't. SORRY BUT I WILL)

4 May
In aft go with Jean to Opera House to see "CHU CHIN CHOW." Fair acting (For THEM) In eve listen to Band Waggon also damn good especially Arthur Askey. I must remember him. VERY HAPPY.

11 June
Go to Scouts. Pass cooking test and am able to eat it!!

15 Sept.
It seems War is very close. Go back to school. In seniors now. Lower 4B. Lousy Day. Outlook LOUSIER.

19 Oct.
  In the morn to school I went
  In learning lessons time was spent!
  In the aft with father dear
  We went to the Ritz, hurray to see-er
  Two films, "Blockade" and "Break The News"
  On which father and I had different views.

"Blockade" was good and that's no wonder
Maddeleine Carrol and Henry Fonda.

30 Oct.
Today was the day in which I wore
Long trousers which I do adore.
It is a day that's in my history
To wear long trousers was a mystery.
To School I went Oh in the morn
And people said "Look what he's got orn"
I staid to Tea and had some fun.
Yes I am still quite young, quite young.

17 Dec.
To School. First performance of "H.M.S. Pina-
fore." Play Little Buttercup. Everything O.K.
except my earings dropped off. Very successful,
plenty of congrats. Home at 10. Joan leaves. very
very sorry, going to be married, like her better
than any other maid. Very sad.

27 Dec.
Go to pantomime at Tonbridge. NOT very good.
NOT very funny. Have a flickin headache, over-
eating, and am finally sick and so rotten I go to
bed.

1939 shows an increasing self-consciousness. This is particularly noticeable in my horror at having to play Titania in the Scout Concert. This was very hard, as the Scout Master had promised me a man's role after Little Buttercup and the "blinkin" girl's part in the previous year's play. But my voice had not yet broken. On the actual day of performance, dreading my father's reaction to my playing the Queen of the Fairies, I purposely blackened my feet, moved like a cart-horse, and got more laughs than Bottom.

The entries show an increase of frightful schoolboy humour—and there is a good deal of code, which I cannot now decipher.

14 Jan.
Go to T.W. with Pop and Jean on my bike which is much too small for me and rotten. Jean and Dad in car. I hang on—till one of Englands wonderful Bobbys stoped us ("Huh you didn't know that hanging on vehicles is against the law?"—Pop "Quite Frankly I didn't oooo) Anyway go to Kenwards bike shop and choose a knew bike. Damn pleased. Ride Home on it Though Pouring. Break my Record Straight away 13 min. Clean it in eve.

20 Jan.

Father reminscing the days of his Youth, (Birp)
Very Pitiful But Honestly I cant help it.

23 Jan.

My Hobbies.

Music, great ear for it (Short Sharp Belch)
This Diary.

Acting. love it. course you know I'm gonna be an
actor.

26 Jan.

MY TYPICAL FATHER.

A topical Joke of his "I saw Mr so and so this
morning, he said you weren't fit to live with a
pig. I said you were!"—Well . . .

30 Jan.

After being careless—Dad said I will kill myself
if I wasn't more careful (And if I do kill myself
It'll be my own fault Anyway. Not pa's or anyone elses for that matter)

31 Jan.

Scout Concert Practice till 5.30. FED UP WITH
IT. Bloody old Titania! Well . . . wouldn't
you be. (Unemployed still restless. There'll be
trouble—I think)

5 Feb.

> *Life Continues*
> *Time never Stops*
> *Strugles unceasing*
> *Victories and Flops.*

8 Feb.

Pa and Ma and me go to Ritz and see Bernard Shaw's "Pygmalion."—In my opinion best British film of last year. Damn Funny. Leslie Howard was suited to his role of "Prof. Higgins." Lovely acting. Catchy Phrases—(you squashed Cabbage Leaf) and Wendy Hiller as Eliza Doolittle who was made from a Cockney (No Bloody Fear) girl into a lady passed as a princess. Very Nerve Racking scenes, when she is in public. Also "King of Alcatraz"

23 Feb.

School and Rehearsal then home at 6 to find we have a TELEVISION SET cost 50 gns. Terribly clear No interference. See a fight between Eric Boon and Arthur Denahar. Best thing ever televised. Damn good fight. See terribly plainly and if I hadn't got such a damn headache I'd tell you more. Don't go to bed till 11.15. Tired out.

24 Feb.

Dress rehearsal of Scout Concert. Blasted awful.

Flickin frock. Wet Wig AND NO shoes or socks.
Still goes all right except that I burst out laughing in Very serious part. (A Restless tense peace
over Europe)

25 Feb.
Skinners School Scout Concert. "Romance of Bot-
tom the Weaver" Me Rotten Awful part. Awful
Acting. Pygmalion Play.

19 April
8.45 start on bike for Hastings. Lovely warm ride
Hastings 2 hours 20 min. Father astounded—Me
not (cough) Conceited Sod. Ma, Pa and Jean
came down by car. Go to pictures with grandma
and grandpa see Shirley Temple (scorn) in "Just
around the corner" Very fair. get flickin headache. (Roosevelt makes speech against Hitler and
Europes growing insanity).

21 May
Long piano practice in eve and then the future
great actor who will surpass:—Henry Irving,
Martin Harvey, Henry Ainley and even Spencer
Tracy (screams of laughter) went to bed.

27 June
1st Exam for Tunbridge Public School Scholar-

ship. Pa is counting on me AND I haven't got a chance. May God help me. (My little crisis)

1 July
  "Why is a dog like a tin of condensed milk?"
  "I don't know."
  "Neither rides a bike . . ."

26 July
Father takes me by car to London. To Palladium Theatre to see "Band Waggon." Terrific Variety Show. All my favourites in the flesh. Arthur Askey not quite as good as on wireless. He's a very little man for the Palladium. Tommy Trinder, a new artist lately gaining fame, was the life of the show. DAMN GOOD. Terrific scenery. Terribly lavish. Damn good seats. Six-shilling ones!!! THANK YOU FATHER.

1 Sept.
Apply for work at the Assembly Hall where Repertory Company is appearing. No luck. Then down to station to see evacuees arriving.
(Hostilities begin in Poland. Germany bombing Civilian Towns and trains full of women and children)

3 Sept.
WAR DECLARED ON GERMANY! 15 minutes after Declaration Air Raid Warning!!!!!! Noth-

ing happened—then later was found to be friendly craft!!!! MY WORD. Everyone in good spirits. June and Jill Creamer come in aft., as our refugees.

4 Sept.
In morn cycle over to Harris. Don't know quite what to do.

6 Sept.
7.0 clock—AIR RAID WARNING. Cor chase my aunt fanny round the gas works! Women from next door come in. AND—in the midst of all Timmy, the cat, has 4 kittens behind the desk in Pops study. Cor blistering blimey! No more excitement—just a dull day.

5 Nov.
Pop takes us to Reminise(?) in Pembury. Walk round all old places. Nice, except Pop gets one of those quick bursts of temper (cough)

13 Dec.
See Rep. Comp, do "Candida" bit above me but very good.

25 Dec.
MERRY CHRISTMAS Goodwill to all men etc (more ships sunk, more people bombed, more

fighting . . .) Anyway we had a good time eating! . . . (I can't find words for my sarcasm)

31 Dec.
May God Save the World Once More.

———

The entry in my diary about the policeman—when I was riding my bike and hanging on to my father's car—is especially interesting. Not recorded in the diary—when the policeman signalled us to halt—was my father's hurried instruction for me to keep quiet and let him do the talking. My father was an experienced driver and knew very well that we were in the wrong. It was the first time I heard him lie (perhaps, on reflection, it was the only time) and it astounded me. It was one of the very few times that I was aware of any weakness in him. To me he had no need to defend himself to anybody.

Perhaps if he had been a weaker man, I would have been less in awe of him, and would have felt a greater freedom in my own life. Perhaps he was much weaker than I imagined, and perhaps I invested him with a heroic strength and integrity. Perhaps his intense desire for me to become a "real boy" and his emphasis on the qualities of courage and truth (in any matter of doubt he would snap out, "Right is right and wrong is wrong") covered up fears and inadequacies of his own. I shall never know. He never spoke of his own struggle to grow up in a household of women—his father was away travelling most of the time—or of the conflict that he must have had in order to achieve his own independence. I did not think him a perfect human being, but I was sure he was a perfect man—a "real man"—and he gave me no peace.

In the evening, when his car came down the drive, electrical interference could be seen on our new television set. It disturbed the tranquil picture. It was him.

I sat up straight. I considered whether the programme we were watching would appeal to him. I considered, according to the time, whether or not I had better dash off to bed. I wondered whether he was tired and cross, elated and excitable, or sentimental and emotional. His chair was vacated. We always gave him the full attention he demanded—whatever his mood—whenever he came home—whether it was from shop or pub. My mother would hide her knitting or her books—he hated to see her read or knit—and hurriedly tidy the room; he might call it a pigsty. If he shouted out the moment he came in the front door, all was probably well. But if there was silence—beware! This would probably mean instructions to "Turn that damned thing off and entertain me!"

In theatrical terms my father was a "star" and the rest of us had to "play as cast," according to his mood, whatever supporting roles he required.

When the time was right we called him "Mr D," or sometimes because of his restless energy, "the Diesel." His nicknames for us were frequently biblical. He would call my mother "the Angel," and he was fond of telling her that she was divinely beautiful and then quickly modify the praise with "if I look quickly" or "in this dim light." My sister would be "the Blessed Lamb," and he sometimes called me "my little Jesus boy"—which implied perhaps that I was the son of God. He certainly seemed to think that he had divine powers.

When I was ill he would come into my bedroom and tell me that he was going to perform a miracle. He would lay his hand on my forehead and say "Give me your will, my son! Give me your will! Let my strength flow into you!" Then a long silence. I would enjoy the confident feeling of his hand on my head, and watch his face turn slightly scarlet and his eyes assume a milky saint-like quality. After a few minutes he would ask if I felt better, and I would murmur that I felt very peaceful and would like to sleep.

59

My father tiptoed from the room—probably lighting a cigarette the moment he got outside —fully satisfied that he had effected a cure. Even in one's own sick-room he had to be the star.

I mostly associate him with his car—or perhaps again, in theatrical terms—his "vehicle." He was a fine driver and took part in competitive rallies, winning several medals and an inscribed ashtray. (As with my inability to throw a ball or play football, for many years I assumed that I couldn't drive—and didn't actually own a car until I was thirty. This was several years after passing my test, but still I assumed that it must be impossible.) His enjoyment of driving was delightful. It gave him an independence he required—and a means of holding his own with snobbish associates in Tunbridge Wells. When passing a waiting bus queue, he would often jeer, "Look at the poor!" During the war and petrol rationing he loathed catching a bus, and it seemed unthinkable to the rest of us to picture him lining up with the other villagers and paying his fare. There was a dreadful occasion when our one-time gardener, William, became a bus conductor and treated my father to a "five-penny one." The thought of being in William's debt was terrible to him.

He was perpetually astonished at his success in achieving our comfortable standard of living.

In the evening, having turned on all the lights in the house, he loved to walk with one of us to the farthest corner of the garden, turn round and gasp, "They must be very rich people living here!"

This capacity of appreciation is one of the most precious gifts that he handed on to us. On any journey in the car he was liable to stop and make us look at the countryside, or the sea or the sky. "This is it!" he would say. We would have to stop all conversation and concentrate in silent appreciation of the scene—until he decided that we had had enough and the journey was resumed. On any momentous occasion—when the family was together and there was cause for rejoicing—he would say, "This is it! Savour this moment! Don't let it go!" My sister and I often mocked his orders—especially when he shouted, "This is it," so sternly that we got too nervous to appreciate whatever it was; but we have both tried to remember his trick of capturing a precious moment of time, by isolating it.

My father was fantastically conscious of time. On his fortieth birthday he announced that he was now approaching fifty. He hated to go to bed at night because it meant the end of another day. He was forever asking us what we were going to do with our lives. He loved to alarm us by simulating decrepit old-age, and if he was bored, we often discovered him lying in a chair pretending to be dead.

He once nearly gave me a heart attack from fright. We were looking over an old village church in the twilight. Suddenly, I realised that I was alone—although I hadn't heard him leave the building. Looking up into a niche set high in the wall, I saw a statue which seemed to be in modern dress. It smiled. I screamed, and then realised that it was father, who had somehow managed to climb up while I wasn't looking.

It is strange, in view of his own eccentricity, that he seemed so anxious for me to conform to a pattern. But I think this had to do with the stuffy society around us, and maybe he thought I would not be able to survive in the class-conscious competitive world of the Thirties—which seemed so permanent at the time. And I certainly showed no signs of any particular talent as I played my colourless role of the average schoolboy.

Living in the Royal Borough of Tunbridge Wells, my father was made to feel over-conscious of being "in trade." When he put his mind to it he was a marvellous shopkeeper; but mostly he put his mind to a host of other things, and while I was growing up he embarked on many strange ventures.

He tried to patent a box of matches called "Boxer Matches" because this is what people usually ask for in a tobacconist's. "Ten Players and a box er matches, please?"

At the Silver Jubilee of George V, he had the largest photographs ever made of the Royal couple and sold them to towns and cities for display. (I remember he visited the Prince of Wales at St James's Palace to get permission to do this and afterwards told us he was sure the Prince wore make-up.)

He bought and quickly sold a jig-saw puzzle factory.

He bought a life-size stuffed elephant on wheels, which he hired out to big stores to advertise "Mammoth Sales." (The elephant was very popular with the village children when it was parked outside the house in Pembury.)

He persuaded the minister of the poorly attended Congregational Church in Tunbridge Wells, to announce during his service that on a Sunday, two weeks hence, God had told him that he would have a full church. My father made sure that this was well reported in the local paper. The church was full to overflowing, and crowds heard the service relayed to them on the pavement outside. It was known locally as a miracle. The *Daily Mirror* wrote a story on it with the headline "Minister's Vision Comes True."

He was fascinated by the potential of Chris-

tianity as a practical living force in modern society, and his most extraordinary achievement
was the creation, during the 1939–45 war, of a
"Ministry of Christianity." With the small prof-
its of the pram shop he rented a tiny office at the
end of Whitehall in Parliament Street—within
sight of Westminster Abbey—wrote "Ministry
of Christianity" on the front door, and tried
to interest and unite the Church in this huge
imaginative dream. He hoped to set up a Ministry of Christianity in every town and city in
the country. These were to be run by local
volunteers, with the co-operation of the local
clergy of all denominations, to help in a practical
Christian way the poor, the sick and the home-
less. I still have some of his leaflets. One of them
is headed "Some Advertising Suggestions."

"Make it known that the Ministry of Christianity will not tolerate a town with Unemployment, Slums or Poverty."

"Make it known that Wealth is just as much
bad taste as Poverty."

"Make it known that if a labourer is worthy of
his hire, so should a Hirer be worthy of the
labourer."

And so on.

On another leaflet he instructs:

"Let it be known that you need shop property

for this work—someone will be willing to pay
the rent, rates and lighting."

"Let it be known that you need furniture—it
will be forthcoming."

"Have a contract with your local press. If
you MAKE NEWS—YOU WILL GET FREE
'WRITE-UPS.' "

And on yet another leaflet entitled "The Right
Spirit" he wrote:

"Get people to talk of Christ and Christianity
in a natural way."

He certainly did this. He liked to think of
himself as a publicity man for Christ. (He would
have been wonderful at promotion. When I became an actor and was out of work he would
often beg me to let him handle my career. He
would design a full-page advertisement for the
theatrical weekly *The Stage* extolling my talent
and good looks—and I was terrified that he would
send it in behind my back.)

He was not in any conventional sense a religious man, although he had been brought up
in a hot-house of Victorian religious mania, but
he loved the idea of Christianity and he was
deeply fond of Jesus. Whenever something went
wrong—even as small a thing as knocking over a
glass—he would ask, "Where's Jesus *now?*"
Walking with him in the garden he would point

out a particularly fat red-currant and comment, "Jesus at his best!" And in his last years, whenever he watched the television programme "What's My Line?," he always got very excited in case the Mystery Guest actually turned out to be Jesus—or on one occasion when a saintly-looking lady walked on, he cried, "Oh, I think it's Mrs Jesus!"

This familiarity with God, combined with his chain-smoking, erratic bursts of temper and humour, doubtless puzzled the clergy when he tried to interest them in his project—especially as he usually suggested leaving the office and visiting the nearest pub.

He did not mince his words when he attacked the Church. I have a copy of an astonishing speech he made at a meeting of the clergy of all denominations at Christ's Church, Tunbridge Wells in July 1942. Here is part of it:

"Ask any group of men and you will hear that the Church is treating them and the world situation with a morbid indifference, instead of rising to its tremendous opportunity. We are still getting uninspired utterances of clerical wisdom, wrapped up in phraseology that the ordinary man cannot understand.

"They will tell you that there is pomp and ceremony, palaces and gaudy raiment, inequality within the Church itself, jumble sales where an aspidistra changes hands with a discarded fender —that for the furtherance of God's kingdom. I say that God is so cluttered up in organised religion that in temper men cry out, 'Stand aside, you priests, and let ordinary people catch a glimpse of the Man of Galilee.' That is how ordinary men think and that is why they seek God in the fields."

This speech doubtless cost him many hours of labour but it is not surprising that the priests were not attracted to the red-faced pram shop keeper.

The Ministry of Christianity gained a little support—but the Church was wary of its obvious Socialist leanings and the Socialists soon became impatient with the Church.

My father eventually closed the London office and returned to the pram shop. Of course, he made a few loyal disciples; and indeed one of them, an octogenarian bicycle-riding parson called Fred, ran a branch in Tunbridge Wells. But the spirit had gone out of it and eventually poor Fred fell off his bike and died.

With the election of the 1945 Labour Government my father changed his interest to local politics and tried to break the Conservative hold on the Royal Borough. He smoked and drank more and frequently wondered at the lack of co-operation he had received from his friend Jesus during those brave days in Parliament Street, when, amidst the Ministries of War, Food, Labour, and Fuel and Power, he had sat in a tiny office, neglecting his family and business, and dreamed a glorious dream.

This was the man I knew best in the world and with whom I had to compete. This was the man with whom I knew it was impossible to compete. Consciously or unconsciously, I had no confidence in my ability to deal with the real world. It seemed as if my father had an impossible glamour and strength and lived and dealt in a world of impossible complexity. I could never be his "real boy" or battle with his "real world." Certainly, I could never rival his "real-life" star quality—and, certainly, I couldn't settle for less.

Make-believe was the only answer. The unreal world of the theatre, where the words and actions are not your own and where you, yourself, do not assume responsibility for what you say and do. I had been drawn towards it since I knew of its existence—although until that summer of 1939 there had been no "straight theatre" in Tunbridge Wells. Up until then I had always imagined myself as a film star. Cycling home from school there was a little hill near Rusthall Common where I used to rest and day-dream. Day-dreams of arriving in Hollywood, of starvation, and eventual discovery. But with the coming of the repertory company to Tunbridge Wells, and visits to plays in London, the dream seemed much nearer home. As the time to leave school approached, I knew that I must confront my father and reveal something of myself to him.

———————

The first two years of the war were my last two years at school. On the morning that war was declared, my father took me into the garden and under the medlar tree—as that first air-raid warning sounded—told me that it was up to us "to set an example to the women." However, "the women" appeared totally unconcerned and were calmly getting lunch—and our cool performance was frustrated. Until the Battle of Britain, which was fought above us in Southern England, the war made very little difference to our lives. At school, air-raid shelters were dug under the playing field and we spent much of the following summer running to them. There were gas masks and there was the black-out.

In 1940, because of air-raids, my father decided that for safety the family should split up and we left "Red Tiles" for several months. The house was let to an elderly couple. My mother looked after the East Grinstead shop and lived in a flat nearby; my sister went to boarding school; and my father and I went into digs opposite his shop in Tunbridge Wells.

It was a very miserable time.

When we visited my mother on early closing day or Sundays, my father often behaved abominably and there were dreadful sulks and violent bursts of temper. I think he was jealous that my mother missed her children more than her life with him, and I found myself—at the age of fifteen—in the position of a rival. He must have been very lonely and frustrated.

Life in the digs was claustrophobic and I had to share a double bed with him. The house was next door to the Public Baths, the owner was the Superintendent of the Swimming Pool, and at least I enjoyed the freedom of an early morning swim before it was opened to the public. The family was very cosy; there was an adored canary and endless games of whist. But there was only the cold bedroom for any privacy in which to work or read.

I had become a voracious reader and spent a lot of time at the Public Library. I particularly enjoyed Dickens, H. G. Wells, J. B. Priestley, and Sinclair Lewis. I also started to read Shakespeare.

70

In a notebook covering my reading during this period there are some lofty comments:

"Crazy Pavements." Beverley Nichols. Weak story with occasional sparkle.

"Dr Faustus." Christopher Marlowe. Good attempt.

"Boswell's Life of Johnson." Fair—rather long winded.

"Faerie Queen." Spenser. Damned boring and damned slow.

"Julius Ceasar." Shakespeare. Fair.

"Paradise Lost." Milton. Beautiful writing but the idea is lost.

"Tarzan of the Apes." E. R. Burroughs. I confess I loved it.

"As You Like It." Shakespeare. Badly constructed.

"The Water Gypsies." A. P. Herbert. Rather cheap in places.

"Wuthering Heights." E. Bronte. Wonderful, beautiful and inspired.

The discovery of this varied world of literature made school life—which now included taking part in the Officers Training Corps and "Digging for Victory"—more endurable.

Nevertheless I was longing for the end of those interminable classes of Mathematics, Physics and Chemistry. I was skilfully humiliated by the Chemistry Master—whom I nicknamed Captain Bligh—when he asked me whether a ton of coal is heavier than a ton of feathers. Of course a ton of coal is heavier! I was tormented by something called "pi squared," and found it impossible to explain a drawing of a square-shaped steak and kidney pie which was discovered in my maths book.

John Gower and I continued our strange friendship. We devised a new and dangerous game called "Kissing the Lady." It meant going into the Hall during lunch-hour, when it was out of bounds, and kissing the portrait of a particularly beady-looking nun which hung on the wall amidst a dreary collection of Renaissance reproductions. We did this because we knew it would be impossible to explain our actions if we were caught. Since the headmaster's study overlooked the Hall, it was a reckless undertaking and we thoroughly enjoyed it. There was no other reason for the game except to court danger.

We also adopted a new friend who intrigued us both. He was a Catholic—which was interesting—and he had a sense of humour even filthier than ours—which was amazing. But from time to time, because of his religious convictions, he would reform and appear to be completely deaf to our sexual chatter. Then, suddenly, he would succumb to temptation and astonish us both with his fertile imagination. He was called "Screw," John Gower was called "Churn," and I was called "Squeaker." We were a great comfort to one another—though they got rather bored with my impressions of Charles Laughton in *Mutiny on the Bounty*, and the everlasting *Clive of India*.

My visits to the cinema continued and there was now the newly built "Assembly Hall," where I could see seasons of repertory, touring plays, variety and Sunday concerts. On a Monday afternoon after school, I made a lengthy front-of-house inspection of the theatre and the cinemas, looking at the photographs and breathless to know the following week's attractions. But the greatest events of those last years at school were two visits to London.

On the first occasion I cycled there and back —taking in Westminster Abbey and a matinee of *The Devil's Disciple* with Robert Donat and Roger Livesey—leaving my bike padlocked outside the Piccadilly Theatre. I got home at 9.15 p.m. after a ninety-mile ride.

On the second occasion, my father took me for a marathon outing, visiting Madame Tussaud's in the morning, Michael Redgrave in *Thunder Rock* in the afternoon, and my first intimate review, *New Faces*, in the evening. As I listened to the glamorous Judy Campbell singing "A Nightingale Sang in Berkeley Square," I was

73

intoxicated with excitement and knew that London must eventually be my home.

———————

We moved back to "Red Tiles" in the spring of 1941 and I left school in July. Sometime around then my father and I had "the talk." We were out walking in the fields.

I told him that I didn't want to go into the pram-shop business and that I was determined to become an actor. Of course he was not entirely surprised by this—he knew well enough my love of the theatre and cinema—but he was nevertheless disappointed for himself and worried for me. He talked of his desire to pass the business on to me and my sons. He wondered why he had worked so hard all these years. He said that it had all been for me—and that he had hoped that I would take it off his shoulders. He then started to worry about my innocence and ignorance. He told me that I was a country boy and would be out of my depth in a drama school; that the other students would be so much more sophisticated. He asked me if I was aware of my ugly Kentish accent. He was worried by my round shoulders and bad sight. He wondered where I got the idea that I had any talent.

74

I held my ground and begged him to let me try my luck. I told him that I had no interest in business (he spoke of Duncan's Pram Shop as if it was Krupps) and that I was confident that I would be able to earn my living as an actor. I think this was his chief worry. He knew that it was an overcrowded profession and he didn't want me to starve.

Finally he realised that my mind was made up and then, typically, his mood changed and he became more excited than I was at the prospect of a life in the theatre. By the time we got home to tell my mother, it had become *his* decision and he was enthusiastically planning my career. He suggested that I call myself Alec as he said that Alexander—my real name—would look too long on playbills and be too expensive in lights.

We wrote to the Royal Academy of Dramatic Art and applied for an entrance test. When the list of audition pieces arrived, my father disapproved of my choice of a comic speech of Professor Higgins from *Pygmalion*, and he started to learn a much more dramatic piece— de Stogumber's hysterical outcry from *St Joan*. To impress me he would burst into snatches of this—rolling his eyes, clasping his hands and calling upon God to forgive him. I cautiously stayed with Professor Higgins and the house reverberated with Shaw; but it seemed as if he would even out-do me as an actor.

However, he did not follow me to RADA on the day of the audition and I passed the entrance test without any trouble—without even doing *Clive of India* as an encore.

I was round-shouldered, flat-chested and be-spectacled. In addition to this, during the summer holidays, my sister and I had both become mysteriously ill with a spinal fever. She had no after-effects, but I was left with a slight paralysis on my left side. For the first year at drama school I walked with a limp and was unable to run, jump, or stand on tip-toe. It is amazing that I was accepted—but it was war-time and they were grateful to recruit any male students—even a shy, stooping, short-sighted, self-conscious son of a shop-keeper—aged sixteen years and four months.

On the morning I left home, we visited my father's parents—now living in Tunbridge Wells. They were horrified that I had inherited my mother's theatrical past and were in great distress that the "little rascal"—that I had played so successfully—had actually grown up into a black sheep. Family prayers were held. My grandfather laid his hand on my head and prayed that God would protect me. My grandmother wept. It was a rather dismal send-off—although as we left the house my grandfather conceded,

"There must be SOME good men even in THAT profession."

My father came with me to London and took me to my room at the YMCA in Tottenham Court Road. Then we went for a walk and, before leaving, he gave me two pieces of advice.

He pointed to a heavily made-up lady in the street and asked me if I knew what she was. I didn't know. He told me she was a prostitute. I was most intrigued. Then he warned me of the dangers of venereal disease—about which I had never heard—and said that at my age it wasn't worth it.

Then he turned to the care of my bowels. He said that the care of the bowels was the beginning of wisdom. He said that I should strive for regularity and finally told me to aim for a daily goal: "Two six-inch coils with a ten-second interval."

We both laughed until he began to cry. Then he hugged me and said goodbye.

At last I was alone.

London in October 1941 had survived the worst air-raids but there was wreckage everywhere. In my own small world the London Central

YMCA had been bombed and only part of it was inhabitable, and the large theatre of the Royal Academy of Dramatic Art was in ruins. I don't remember any apprehensions about my safety when I started life in the big city, only a natural timidity about meeting my fellow students —most of whom were older than I—and a great fear of being laughed at when I was called upon to perform in front of them.

Arriving at the Academy on the first morning, the great shock was encountering so many girls. According to my diary: "Breakfast and then to RADA . . . am immediately subdued by the appearance of Les Girls—precocious, effusive and intimidating. Shrieks of 'Darling!' rend the air. Join the other males who are equally subdued. We, the juniors, consist of 8 men and 30 girls, and throughout the morning we read a play by Noel Coward. I have a prolonged love scene and frantically propose to an unseen girl on the other side of the room." It was obviously quite different from Maths at Skinners School. At the end of the day I wrote: "Go for a walk. See London in the moonlight, and am suddenly superbly happy. I am a student and live up in town, and everything's fine."

(Of course the enormous predominance of girl students made casting very difficult for the teachers. There was a particularly hilarious production of *Anthony and Cleopatra* with one Anthony and thirteen Cleopatras. The startled expression on Anthony's face as the succession of Cleopatras entered—some tall, some short, some fat, some thin—was very funny.)

On the second day, to celebrate my independence, I went on the underground for the first time and treated myself to "an excellent cheap seat" at the New Victoria Cinema. My choice was Walt Disney's *Reluctant Dragon*.

I spent my first weekend alone in London going to see a very English family play, *Quiet Weekend*—which made me feel rather homesick—and, on the Sunday, going to church at St Martin's in the Fields in the morning, and to a concert at the Albert Hall in the afternoon. After the concert, while looking at the Albert Memorial, I was picked up by a middle-aged gentleman who took me for a meal in the Edgware Road. He then suggested going back to his flat. He was concerned about my limp and said that he would like to examine my thigh muscles. I refused his kind offer and returned to the comparative safety of the YMCA—feeling worldly wise and inaccessible.

Being a gaunt sixteen-year-old, I was not given heroic parts and, in the end-of-term production, played the seventy-five-year-old father in Dodie Smith's family play *Dear Octopus*. My hands were heavily veined with blue grease-paint and my hair gave off clouds of white powder each time I kissed a member of my family, but I was prevented from blacking out my teeth. I moved with that strange loping deportment—more like an elderly ape—that is usually adopted by inexperienced young actors when challenged by a "character" part.

My parents came to see me and my father regretted that I had not had a death scene since I appeared to be so close to it. He also invited me to repeat the son's speech—about the family being a "dear octopus"—at our own Christmas festivities at home. I never did this, although he frequently asked me in succeeding years. Instead I priggishly learnt the first chapter of Genesis and thoroughly confused my religious grandparents—who actually thought that actors sang rude songs in Music Halls. My grandmother always asked me what songs I had been singing. They had never seen a play.

I now began to see plenty; and I began to take part in those wildly intolerant discussions common to all drama students. The best part of the day was when the classes were over and groups of us gathered for tea at Taylor's Café in Tottenham Court Road. I would smoke—in an attempt to look older. I didn't say very much, but learnt a trick of raising one eyebrow and looking as if I was continually suppressing a witty remark. Luckily I was not often asked to express one of them.

As a student I made little progress—although I found sympathetic teachers in Litz Pisk and Colin Chandler—but I was too young and callow, and my body, weakened by the spinal fever, would not do as it was told. My attempts at mime were a disaster. I was finally excused it, and accompanied the exercises of other students by playing the piano. I couldn't fence. And my ineptitude at improvisation nearly led to expulsion. The Principal, Sir Kenneth Barnes, came to watch a class. We were a group of spies and I was sent to steal "the papers." Returning without them, the others cross-examined me. Had I looked everywhere? Had I searched every drawer? "Yes," I replied nervously, "I even searched his secretary's drawers." There was a moment's silence and then I started to laugh uncontrollably and was asked to leave the room. I have never cared for improvisation.

The Shakespeare classes were also very frightening, and I got a shock when my friend David Ashman impersonated my false, rich deep voice and my attempts to stretch myself to a great height. Like many young actors, I couldn't believe that Shakespearean characters were actu-

ally human beings. I thought they were giant
poetry-speaking robots.

Despite the fact that I wasn't really very good
in any of the classes, it didn't worry me. There
was no hurry. I had a steely core of confidence
deep down inside me. I knew that my progress
would be gradual and that I must absorb everything that could be learnt along the way. Nothing else interested me.

But I enjoyed my first friendships with kindred spirits. It was a great relief to be among
young people with the same interests and am-
bitions.

There was Betty Oughton, who invited me to
her home in Sutton for the weekend and breath-
lessly played me a record of a new singer called
Frank Sinatra.

There was a wonderful little Scots girl—Jean
Howison—with a tremendous talent and a caus-
tic tongue, who loved to shock me. She shared a
large rambling flat near Olympia, where I often
used to stay the night. There were informal
parties where we drank beer, ate macaroni
cheese, mimicked our elders and talked endlessly. I don't remember what we talked about.
The only sentence that I can recall was by a
student who had got his first part in a film.
"Now I shall never be able to eat in Lyons
again."

Then there was the brilliant, humorous Peter
Geary—who lived in South London and amazed
me by his ability to mock his own suburban
background. He and I planned to act, direct and
write plays together. We also did impersonations of the Music Hall team, Murray and
Mooney.

"I can't do it. You can't do it. Lloyd George
can't do it."

"Do what?"

"Milk chocolate!—Ere." etc.

Peter Geary was a joyous companion and a
richly gifted human being. He died—as he bit-
terly predicted in a letter—"with a poppy up his
arse," during the last months of the war.

The senior pupils included Harold Lang,
Richard Attenborough, and Miriam Brickman.
They had an impossible glamour for us, and
when I met any of them after our Academy days
I was still dreadfully shy and tongue-tied.

I adored living in London, but the smell of
disinfectant at the YMCA began to depress me
and I moved to a room at the Interval Club.
This was a small Catholic Theatrical organisa-
tion—mostly used by elderly actors and actresses.
I had a tiny bedroom with a little balcony on
the top floor of the annexe in Soho Square, and
my breakfast tray was brought to me in bed.

This was the life.

During the Easter holidays we did a short school's tour of *Julius Caesar*—in which I can only remember giggling. But my first professional engagement was during the 1942 summer vacation, when I answered an advertisement in *The Stage* and was offered work with a weekly repertory company in Macclesfield. The company was run by a lady, and in her letter to me she wrote: "This confirms your engagement —Stage manager and parts, £3 per week. Half salary during rehearsal week. Will let you have a formal contract on arrival if you desire it."

In those days an actor was expected to provide his own wardrobe for all contemporary plays, so I packed my mother's old theatrical skip— borrowing my father's dinner jacket, some moth-eaten jodhpurs, morning clothes and a pin-striped suit, bought some make-up from Mr Spaan in Lisle Street—and, with my bicycle in the luggage van, got on the train for Macclesfield. I arrived on a wet Saturday afternoon, left my belongings at the station and searched unsuccessfully for digs.

In the evening I went to the theatre and saw the company perform. In Henry James' words —describing Irving's Macbeth—"I sat through the performance in a sort of melancholy amaze-

ment." Never before had I seen this sort of acting, and I realised that my year's training at
RADA was not going to be much help. The actors seemed to shout everything, face out front,
and signal to the audience whenever there was a
good laugh line. What depressed me further was
the fact that the audience seemed to love it, and
applauded every exit made through the flimsy
ill-fitting doors. The theatre had a suffocating
smell of unwashed bodies. I spent a sleepless
night at the Macclesfield Arms Hotel.

Eventually I found digs with a dear lady
called Grace Smith, who charged me thirty-
seven shillings and six pence a week with full
board and, although I protested, she used to give
me back two shillings and six pence every week
for extra pocket money.

It was a splendid introduction to the theatre.
Apart from my Assistant Stage Manager, Joyce
Thornton, there was no stage staff and I had to
do every job imaginable—as well as playing a
series of unlikely roles. The director, Arthur
Dallas, taught me everything from tying a cleat
to mascaraing my eye-lashes. I collected furniture
and props from shops and friends of the theatre,
and pushed a laden handcart through the hilly
streets of the town. There were no dressing-
rooms—only a curtained partition under the
stage to separate the men and women. As there

were no wash basins, I collected two buckets of
water from the pub next door for the actors and
actresses before the performance each night. I
changed the scenery, worked the switchboard,
pulled the curtain up and down, and in the
lunch hour sometimes sold tickets in the box-office. On Sundays, I cleaned up the previous
week's play, swept the stage and helped to paint
the flats for the coming attraction. If it was a
heavy production with more than one set, all the
men in the company would help with the scene
changes, and when Joyce and I were on stage,
Arthur Dallas would run the show from the
wings.

My first play was *Paddy the Next Best Thing*
which included a scene in a railway carriage.
The local paper wrote: "Compliments to Alec
McCowen and Joyce Thornton on their scenic
efforts. The train journey is most realistic." We
were thrilled. However, my performance as
Micky, the lovable old man-servant, was not
mentioned.

There was a rough-tongued character actor of
the old school in the company, and despite my
RADA background—which was regarded as a
joke—he seemed fond of me. Whenever he passed
me by—lugging buckets, pushing the cart or
stacking scenery—he would quietly ask: "Do
you think you'll like the profession?"

For much of the time I hated it. I would try
to anaesthetise myself and pretend that it was
happening to someone else; that I would be waiting on the railway station platform at the end of
the job, to be joined by this hardened labourer.

But I was also exhilarated by the sense of
power that I felt on the stage. I was fast becoming seduced by my own exit rounds and I began
to persuade myself that it was a marvellous company. In my final week they gave me the hon-
our of making the curtain speech. "Thank you
for your wonderful reception. Next week the
company will present such and such." The play
ended in a tableau and then we moved into line
to take our bows. I stepped forward centre stage,
made the speech and stepped back into line.
There was a long pause. The applause gradually
died down, and then, realising that there was no
one in the wings to pull down the curtain, I
shuffled off. The moment of glory was quickly
over.

Soon the six weeks in Macclesfield were over.
I met my sensitive other half on the station platform, and we travelled safely home in buoyant
high spirits. My father, noticing my newly
found confidence and wanting a part in it, said:
"You think you're everybody just because you're
my son . . ."

It is true that for the first few years acting was

really an excuse to "show off." The colourless
schoolboy and the agreeable son, who had played
a supporting role to a starring father, was suddenly let loose. Once rehearsals were over and
there was no more directorial authority, I sniffed
freedom and displayed my astonishing self for
certain approval. Fear of an audience was
quickly over—and the audiences I played to in
those early years seemed very easily pleased.

In a Repertory Company there is no competition. You know where you are and who you are
from the moment your contract is signed. You are
the only one of your type. You are a big fish in a
small pond—and the pond seems like an ocean.
It is highly enjoyable and a little unbalancing.

Having had a taste of glory at Macclesfield, I
decided to leave RADA without completing the
course. There was also the likelihood of my being called up into the forces when I was eighteen. I left the Academy after one more term.

My final appearance was in a public performance of *A Midsummer Night's Dream*. This has
never been a lucky play for me. After the Scout
Concert Titania with the dirty feet, I now gave a
nose-bleeding Lysander. The bleeding started
just before I went on stage and I acted with my
head in the air, sniffing hard between speeches
and looking like an afflicted camel. On my end-
of-term report the Principal remarked, "Has

promise, but thinks too much of himself." (Years later, at the Old Vic, in another ill-fated production, I crashed my shin, broke a blood-vessel and played Oberon with a limp.)

When the term ended there was a short students' tour of one-act plays by Chekhov and Thornton Wilder. We were booed in Ecclefechan and bombed in Grimsby. Then I left the competition of my contemporaries.

———————

While playing at Macclesfield there was great excitement one night when a Northern impresario, who ran several repertory companies, came to the play. The following day the leading lady told me that I had been "spotted," and that if ever I needed work to get in touch with him. I now did this, and was engaged as a character-juvenile with the Manchester Repertory Company temporarily resident at Rhyl in North Wales. During my three months with them I also played in *Little Women* with a twin company on the pier as Llandudno.

My salary was £5.10 a week and I opened a Post Office Savings Account. My digs were on the front over an amusement arcade, and the landlady gave me a custard pie every day for tea. I have never been able to eat a custard pie since.

The time approached for my Army Medical Test, and on a free afternoon I climbed the Great Orme at Llandudno and solemnly pondered Conscientious Objection. I recorded my conclusion in my diary. "Anyone who has cut and dried principles in this chaotic world is a fool." I didn't pass the Medical owing to my bad sight and the lingering results of spinal fever, and returned reflectively to Rhyl. The standard of the company seemed very low and I thought I could do better, so I gave in my notice and went home.

Now began my first experience of unemployment and agents. It was a sobering experience, for even with the acute man shortage it was difficult for me to find work.

I nearly joined Donald Wolfit, who interviewed me briefly in his dressing room. Without any preamble he asked me to roll up my trouser leg and show him my calf. I did so. He offered me Stage Manager and Walk On. I refused.

I wrote "job letters" to the more select repertory companies, and went for interviews at places like Oxford and Windsor. But in order to hide my nervousness I developed an impossibly hearty interview manner, and tried to make things easier for the director or manager by speaking for them and turning myself down before they had a chance to do so. "I'm sure I'm just wasting your time," I would say. "Your company is bound to be full, and I have very little experience anyway." They looked very relieved, thanked me for coming, said they would remember me, and forgot me before I had left the room.

The weeks rolled on and I felt my father's fears would be realised. The humiliation was intensified because of the war and the feeling of uselessness. I felt a failure both as a young man and an actor, and wrote despairingly in my diary: "Oh Christ above, look down on me." But eventually an agent called Nora Nelson King befriended me. She got me an interview with Geoffrey Staines, the director of a fine company at the Theatre Royal, York. I managed to curb my tongue and he engaged me as Assistant Stage Manager and to play small parts. This was my home for the next eighteen months. My father called me "the York Ham."

Theatrical landladies have almost disappeared. Nowadays, with frozen foods and laundrettes, young actors can look after themselves. But my days in rep are coloured by the many bedsitters I ate and slept in, and the many ebullient landladies who looked after me.

At first I lived with Mrs Meadows and then I moved to Mrs Lythe. Annie Lythe was a superb, vivacious Yorkshirewoman, and, in addition to looking after the lodgers and her own family, she was free for midwifery and laying out the dead. At lunch she would bring in a crisp Yorkshire pudding with succulent onion gravy as a starter, and tell me details of her latest birth or death. Her little home was renowned as a great theatrical boarding house. Emlyn Williams always stayed in her first floor front, and I was often told when she brought in my breakfast that I had slept in Phyllis Calvert's bed— "So you've got something to live up to!" She came to the first night every Monday and gave me notes before I went to bed. Once, after I thought that I had given a wonderful performance, she said: "Well, you made a proper fool of yourself tonight!" The director confirmed this in the morning. I was joined at meal-times by another ASM, Mary Gunn, who suffered my table manners for many months.

At first there was no acting for me, and I endured the drudgery of stage-management under the rigid discipline of a great theatrical tyrant called Norman Hoult. He taught me to prompt. He taught me to set cups and telephones so that the actors could best pick them up. He insisted on my emptying ash-trays as soon as they were used and, when he discovered me reading Dostoievsky in the prompt corner, he turned white and confiscated the book. At first I loathed him, and then one night I saw him pick up an evening paper and read that the actor Owen Nares was dead. It was as if one of his own family had died. He gasped "God save the King!" and had to sit down for several minutes. The theatre was his life and he imparted some of his single-minded enthusiasm to me.

Eventually I was given parts to play and learnt a great deal from Geoffrey Staines' direction. The weeks sped by and I could walk the mile from the digs to the theatre without once raising my head from the current script. I think this must have been when I memorised my lines because according to my diaries I saw at least two films a week and read at least two books.

I was a rather colourless puritanical personality, defensive and very lonely for much of the time. "Self-conscious gluttony and filth" is how I described a theatre party where there was drinking and a few dirty jokes were told in mixed company. Only on stage, and in writing, did any of my own exuberance break out. I wrote: "love acting, even badly." "Lazily exude charm." "Reading King and Edward Lear." "I'm suffering from obscurity." "Wish I was more precocious out of this diary." And on an occasion when things must have been very dull: "Broke my leg and acted in splints. Fainted just after second house. Everybody very kind."

Sometimes I was given a part that should perhaps have gone to another actor. The most outstanding occasion was during the week of my nineteenth birthday when I played the centenarian in *A Hundred Years Old*. There was a seventy-five-year-old character man in the company who sulked understandably at having to play my son. On the night of my birthday Mrs Lythe made a birthday cake which was handed up over the footlights, and I made a gracious speech of thanks.

It was a very happy time because it was a very busy time, but at the end of eighteen months it seemed as if I should emerge and see something more of the world. We did a short tour of army camps and stayed in Norwich. There, I went to the Maddermarket Theatre and met the producer, Nugent Monck.

The Maddermarket is a copy of an Elizabethan theatre with an apron stage. At the time it seemed a tremendous challenge to act in conditions of such intimacy. Monck, already an almost legendary figure, not only directed amateur productions of all Shakespeare's plays at his own theatre—including a dramatisation of the Sonnets—but also directed Scofield at Stratford and the original production of Wolfit's *Lear*. Eagerly I offered my services and for a few weeks became an amateur. Monck gave me board and lodging and ten shillings a week pocket money. I helped to run his theatre back-stage and played in his production of *Major Barbara*.

He was a sensitive, humorous dictator, and I loved him and his theatre. I also loved his beautiful Elizabethan house which was always full of interesting people; but I couldn't stand the amateurs.

I went home to Tunbridge Wells, did a special week with the rep at the Assembly Hall, and then flew to India.

As a child I had two recurring dreams. One was a dream about Mount Everest, and the other a dream about New York. Mount Everest seemed to be at the bottom of a field in Pembury and I gazed in wonder at its impossible height. New York was more of a nightmare, as all the skyscrapers were very like tall human beings and they utterly overwhelmed me. I think both dreams had to do with my father and the impossibility of competing with him. Strangely, he was instrumental in my seeing these sights before I was twenty-three.

During my time at York, out of a sense of guilt, I had tried to get into the Merchant Navy, but was told again that I was unfit. Now the war was drawing to a close I felt I should try to do

something patriotic. My father suggested that I
joined ENSA and apply for overseas duty, com-
bining my patriotism with an opportunity to see
something of the world. Since this idea also provided an opportunity to impress my father I
asked to be sent as far away as possible, and was
told that a replacement was urgently needed in
the Indian Repertory Company.

My mother had me photographed in my uni-
form; there were various inoculations, and I set
off from the B.O.A.C. terminal at Victoria. Luckily I was accompanied on the journey by another performer, Bob Denzer, a member of a
well-known dancing-skeleton act called Dumarte
and Denzer. Without him I might never have
got there. We changed planes at Rabat and again
in Cairo, where we spent several nights and then
seemed to get completely forgotten in Karachi.
Finally Bob got a lift for both of us on a plane to
Calcutta, where I was informed that the Indian
Repertory Company had been disbanded for the
past three months. This pertinent fact was obviously unknown in London. There was therefore
nothing for me to do.

Understandably I was upset and complained
to Jack Hawkins who was then in charge of
ENSA for that area. He told me that the only
straight play company in India at that time was
a tour of a light comedy called *Love in a Mist*,
and by chance one of the actors was due to go

home. I volunteered to replace him and was put on a train to Gauhati where I was told someone would meet me. I promptly forgot where I was going and had no idea how long it would take. After the first night on the train everybody got off and the luggage was carried to a river. I had breakfast on a ferry crossing the Brahmaputra and continued the journey feeling amazingly carefree. At Gauhati an official told me that the *Love in a Mist* company had already left and was much further north in Dibrugarh near Tibet. I got back on the train.

During the day I was joined in the otherwise empty compartment by a sad-looking Indian and I longed to talk with him. After many hours of travelling through an unchanging countryside of paddy fields and tiny villages of huts, I mustered up my courage and, pointing to the people working in the mud, said, "Do they live like this all their lives?" The Indian surveyed them, sighed enviously and murmured, "What more could you want?" The conversation languished.

The next day I found my new colleagues and quickly took over my part in the play. We toured Assam for a few weeks, returned to Calcutta where we spent V.J. day, and then played in Burma to the newly released prisoners of war. One of these was the fiancé of an actress in the company. They decided to marry immediately and the tour ended.

I waited around in Calcutta hoping for another assignment and developed septic prickly heat. This took the form of blisters on my back and arms. An army doctor prescribed scrubbing my skin with soap and water, but I declined this remedy and asked for leave in the hills. The character lady from *Love in a Mist*, Elsie Orf, who was also waiting for another job accompanied me to Darjeeling.

I adored the little town and the dazzling view of the mountains above the clouds. Like my father turning to gasp at the rich spectacle of his home, I would surprise myself by casually turning round to see the immense valleys, the smaller hills and then, suddenly, the snow in the sky. We went on ponies up Tiger Hill with the other tourists to see the dawn hit Everest and the Himalayas. But then Elsie began to make enquiries about a trek that would bring us much nearer to the highest peak in the world. She found out it was possible and asked me to take charge.

The leading man of *Love in a Mist* nicknamed Elsie Orf "The Tank." She was certainly a strongly built and very determined woman. Aged about fifty, she was a frustrated amateur actress who had seized the opportunity of touring with ENSA not only to act but also to see as much of the world as possible. When it was over she returned to her home in Kingswear, laden with mementoes and memories. Apart from amateur productions she never acted again, and died a few years later.

Today it is hard to believe that the adventure really happened, but Elsie kept a log book and I still have a copy. It is entitled "A TREK ON THE ROOF OF THE WORLD. OCTOBER 1945," and it is dedicated "To Alec, the one ahead, my fellow pilgrim, from his ancient companion Elsie." It records how we bought provisions in Darjeeling, reserved forest bungalows where we could spend the nights, and engaged our team of companions.

We made a quaint little company. There was me; a splendid little Tibetan sirdar—guide and cook—called Lapkah; two Nepalese bearers called Nimpassan and Benoit who carried the food; a little white pony called Tik Tik carrying the bed-rolls; and, gallantly bringing up the rear, Elsie.

Elsie's legs were good but her wind was bad. However she was never more than an hour behind the rest of us. I gaily strode on in front by myself. We preferred it that way, as Elsie's habit of stopping to look at, and often to collect, any rare flower or butterfly along the way became rather wearing.

We drove to the border of Nepal where we were joined by Lapkah and the bearers, and then set off on foot for our first halt at Jorepokri. Two days later we arrived in a blinding snowstorm at Sandakphu, having walked over thirty miles and climbed to a height of nearly 12,000 feet.

Sandakphu consisted of two bungalows, a few huts and a pond. It commands an unparalleled view of the highest mountains in the world to the north, stretching from one end of the horizon to the other, and an unending expanse of the Indian plain to the south, thousands of feet below. At dawn there was the most gorgeous spectacle I have ever seen in my life. The sun came up and hit the peak of Everest and then gradually warmed the white-blue sides of all the mountains with a glowing orange light. The air was fresh and clean and cold, and the night's ice thawed in ten minutes. Alone with this vision I felt drunk with power and shouted loud greetings which were echoed back to me from all directions.

We spent the day in the clouds and it seemed to me as if I was near to glorious revelations, keenly aware of being alive, able for a little while to look down on ambition and frustration and curious endeavour. Released from the family, and belonging to a larger mystery.

We continued the journey walking through forests of bamboo and rhododendron; up precipitous little paths that were apt to crumble down almost vertical slopes into enormous valleys with tempestuous rivers hurtling over stones and rocks; through rather frightening villages full of strange smells, and the squat stocky hill people; along lovely giddy ridges with dark and beautiful forests all around. Sometimes in hot sunshine through the hibiscus and the orange trees. Sometimes in rain or snow, passing umbrella-carrying Gurkha soldiers singing as they walked home from the war to Katmandu.

In the evening, when we were alone in some bleak draughty little forest bungalow, weary after the day's climb, sitting over a log fire, Lapkah would bring us hot water and limes and honey to have with our whisky, and ask about tomorrow's orders. And then in shocking Urdu, I would play the burra sahib and plan a six o'clock start and porridge for breakfast and what we would have for tiffin en route. Then one of the Nepalese bearers, small, greasy, good-humoured and unbelievably strong, would bring in some soaking logs that almost smoked us out of the room, and beg for a cigarette before going to bed.

And in the morning the packing up of bedrolls, and the loading of the pony, the paying of the bungalow chowkidar, and the photograph that Elsie always decided to take just as we were ready to leave.

Breakfast, and Mount Everest seen through a dirty pane of glass.

Lunch, and the distant sound of voices singing tuneless carefree songs in the mountain air.

What more?

—"This is it!"

———————

There was no more work in India, so I came home on a troopship, and arrived in time for Christmas; with my cases full of ornamental elephants, brass ashtrays, a musty copy of *The Decameron* and a disastrous suit made by a Darjeeling Market tailor. For a little while at home I was a hero, and then the struggle for work began again.

Most of my work during the next two years I got through the help of Geoffrey Staines. I played in Perth for six weeks and met John Moffatt whom I call my oldest friend. My twenty-first birthday was spent during a six-month season at the Alexandra Theatre, Birmingham. There was nine months at Scarborough and back again to York. But I was not progressing either as an actor or a human being. I was just becoming an "old pro."

It was while I was at Scarborough that a

strange incident occurred. One night after the play, I left the theatre, walked down the narrow passage from the stage-door to the street, and turned right to go home to my digs. It was dark, but standing across the street was a ghostly figure who looked familiar. I stared for a moment and realised that it was my father. I couldn't imagine what he was doing there, nearly three hundred miles from home. Then I crossed the road and greeted him, and we went and had a drink together. It transpired that he had come to the town on business, but I shall never know if I hadn't noticed him or if I had left the theatre with company whether he would have emerged from the shadows and made himself known to me. The incident has a strange dream-like quality for me, and even now, although he is dead, I keep expecting it to happen again.

———————

Finally I knew the time had come for me to try my luck in London. After a flamboyant performance in one of those popular plays of the time about an afflicted young man who commits murder when the moon is full, I left York for the second time, and by a happy chance got a job almost immediately.

I had taken my mother to see a performance of the play *Edward My Son*. Afterwards, at Charing Cross station waiting for our train back to Tunbridge Wells, we recognised, standing near us, the crusty character actor D. A. Clarke-Smith. He had appeared in the play, and with unusual boldness I accosted him. The conversation went something like this:

"Mr Clarke-Smith?"

"Why?"

"I saw the play tonight and enjoyed your performance very much."

"Thank you."

". . . I'm an actor myself."

"Where do you act?"

"In repertory."

"Where?"

"In the provinces."

"What's the good of that?"

"Well I, er . . ."

"Why don't you act in London?"

"Well I, er . . ."

"You'll have to act in London if you want to get anywhere."

"Well I, er . . ."

"Are you a good actor?"

"Yes I am."

"Come and see me after the matinee on Saturday. I may be able to fix you up with something."

He did fix me up with something. He arranged an audition with the director Peter Ashmore and I was engaged as an understudy in a revival of Shaw's *You Never Can Tell* in which Mr Clarke-Smith appeared. Mr Clarke-Smith actually appeared in two West End plays simultaneously, because he continued his role in the early scenes of *Edward My Son* and then journeyed to Wyndham's Theatre to play in the last act of *You Never Can Tell*. No wonder provincial actors couldn't get work in London! He was a delightful man and, since he lived near Tunbridge Wells, I was able to introduce him to my father, who loved impersonating his rich actor-ish voice.

I was wildly impressed at being connected with a West End play, and stood in awe of the starry cast, but after a few weeks, cooped up in a tiny top floor dressing room, the excitement palled. There seemed very little chance that I would ever appear since my principal was in rude health. Then an intriguing offer came along to join a small company going to Newfoundland.

I was torn between leaving the security of a safe London job, and going back into weekly

repertory—even though it included the novelty
of working across the Atlantic. My father's attitude decided me. I think he regarded my un-
derstudying in the same way that he had regarded my lying in bed in the mornings. "Get
up my son! You're rotting!" He was thrilled at
the opportunity of my going to America and told
me not to come back. At any rate he said that I
should not come home until I had seen as much
of America as possible, and intimated that along
the way I might achieve fame and fortune. I recalled a distant occasion in my schooldays when
my father, bored with my lack of initiative, had
said: "Why don't you run away from home or
something!" So I went to Newfoundland.

———————

By this time I was a very experienced weekly
repertory actor and had played over a hundred
parts; but my approach to a performance was
shallow and arrogant, and my only gift was a
facility in comic timing. I had a tricky talent
for impersonation, with various voices, various
walks and various faces assembled with the aid
of my make-up box. I gave little thought to a
performance which had to be ready after five

morning rehearsals, and by mid-week of playing I often complained of feeling stale. It is true that on each Monday when we dress-rehearsed and opened I often had serious stomach trouble caused by nerves, but on the following day when we assembled to begin the next play all would be well. We would discuss clothes, wigs, make-up, and how to ring the changes on an audience that saw the same actors week after week.

It wasn't until my first trip to America that I realised that acting could be more than impersonation. After the freezing repertory season in St. John's, Newfoundland, I sailed to New York and spent my salary seeing everything possible in the 1948 theatre season. Among the plays was Tennessee Williams' *A Streetcar Named Desire*, directed by Elia Kazan, and in the cast was Marlon Brando. This was the most exciting production that I had ever seen, and here was an actor for my own generation. After the performance I queued at the box-office to get another ticket, wishing to confirm what I had just seen. It was confirmed.

It had never occurred to me to think that I could possibly compete with the great English classical actors. I had seen Gielgud's Hamlet, Olivier's Richard III and Richardson's Falstaff, but these seemed to be superhuman performances, and those actors seemed to belong to another race of men. They had nothing to do with me and I didn't seem to belong to the same profession. If I had any definite dream of the future it was that one day I might wake up and miraculously find myself as a new Rex Harrison or Cary Grant. But when I looked in the mirror at my image this seemed equally unlikely.

With the experience of seeing *Streetcar* I finally found an objective and a sense of direction. This acting was much less forbidding than the cold, efficient, stylised naturalism of the contemporary London theatre. This acting was warm, rich and human, and had a depth and subtlety that I had never seen before. This acting did not rely on appearance, or a knowledge of how to wear a crown or shoot a cufflink. This acting was real—and I had a sneaking suspicion that it was very difficult.

But suddenly I was stage-struck in the real sense. Suddenly I wanted to be involved in the theatre because it fascinated me, and not because it offered a way of avoiding involvement in real life.

I did not stay on in America as my father had suggested, nor did I make my fame and fortune; but at last I realised that I belonged to an exciting and challenging profession, and that it was time for me to start learning my job.

It is obvious that I inherited a love of the theatre
from my mother. It is also obvious that in their
separate ways both of my grandfathers were at
home in front of an audience—either in Church
or Parliament. But I think that my father was
the chief cause of my becoming an actor. As a
child I was overwhelmed by his world and over-
awed by his strength. I tried to escape to an artificial world and hoped to evade responsibility.
But the artificial world turned out to have a complexity of its own, and the responsibility of an
actor is no less because it is concerned with make-
believe. He is responsible to his playwright, his
audience, and to his colleagues. My attempts at
evasion finally failed. Whether I liked it or not
I was my father's son.

It took me a long time to learn that he was not
my enemy; that he wanted my well-being and
my success, and that life was not an act of de-
fiance. It took me a long time to reveal my personality, and to admit my conflicting emotions
of love and hate.

While in repertory I had written six plays—
all of them terrible. The first had the traditional
theme of patricide. It was extremely violent, and
depicted two sons: one of them passive, artistic
and fulfilled; the other aggressive, emotional

and stunted. The aggressive son gleefully mur-
ders his father. The passive son calmly continued his career. With some trepidation I showed
the play to my father. He seemed delighted by
it and roared with laughter. I was amazed.

With the passing years the intensity of the relationship slackened, although I always sought
his good opinion and longed to impress him
with each performance. It is perhaps not entirely
a coincidence that some of these have been un-
conventional religious protesters: the Jesuit in
The Representative, Luther and Hadrian VII.
Perhaps some day there will be a play about a
red-faced pram shop keeper who faced an audience of clergy and cried: "Stand aside, you
priests, and let ordinary people catch a glimpse
of the Man of Galilee."

The last time I saw him was in 1968 before
going on another trip to New York. Owing to
Parkinson's Disease he had lost his sense of bal-
ance and could hardly walk. His speech was almost gone, but before I left he stumbled into the
kitchen, where I was having coffee with my
mother, and painfully asked me if I had enough
money for the journey.

When I drove away he stood at the window in
his dressing-gown and muffler, and feebly at-
tempted to wave goodbye.

I tried to remember that this was the man who

used to conduct the Hallelujah Chorus before leaving for work in the morning; who once called me "the cripple"; who once threw a ball so high that it vanished from my sight . . .

He died nine months later while I was still playing Hadrian VII in New York.

Soon after this Peter Dews asked me to play Hamlet with his company in Birmingham. It seemed a marvellous idea. I felt a natural sympathy for this eloquent and newly bereaved son. But when it came to acting the part I realised that it was a mistake and came to hate the situation.

I hadn't the energy to mourn for someone else's father before I found out how much I wanted to mourn for my own.

That is why there was confusion.

That is why I have written this small book.

This is what I have discovered.

I do not want to mourn my father. But I want to thank him; and wish he could know how I long for his company sometimes.

Alec McCowen was born in Tunbridge Wells, England, and attended, rather briefly, the Royal Academy of Dramatic Art. He has been a member of the National Theatre and the Royal Shakespeare Company, and many of his stage appearances—including the title roles in *Hadrian VII*, *The Philanthropist*, and *The Misanthrope*—have been highly acclaimed in London and New York. Among his films are *Frenzy*, and *Travels with My Aunt*. He has most recently been seen on the American stage with his solo presentation of St Mark's Gospel.